Barry Pickthall

GOING FOREIGN

Cruising Abroad for the First Time

ADLARD COLES NAUTICAL · LONDON

Published by Adlard Coles Nautical
an imprint of A & C Black Publishers Ltd
36 Soho Square, London W1D 3QY
www.adlardcoles.com

First edition published 2010

ISBN 978-1-4081-2675-2

A CIP catalogue record for this book is available from the British Library.
This book is produced using paper that is made from wood grown in managed, sustainable forests. It is natural, renewable and recyclable. The logging and manufacturing processes conform to the environmental regulations of the country of origin.

Typeset in Helvetica Neue
Designed by PPL Ltd
Printed and bound in China by RR Donnelley South China Printing Co'

Acknowledgements

Our thanks go to Tim Bishop and his family, who shared their account and pictures of a memorable 2-week voyage from the Solent to the Frisian Islands and back aboard their Halberg Rassy 36 *Minke II*, and to Gary Fry who also provided advice and pictures following a leisurely 3-month cruise with his wife around Brittany aboard their MG 27 *Jala 2*.

Other valuable contributions toward this book have come from Garmin, Simrad, and HM Customs.

Grateful thanks must also go to PPL's designers Greg Filip and Kara Thomas, and to Rowland Eno and the picture research team at PPL Photo Agency for sourcing the many photographs we needed to illustrate particular points throughout the book.

Design: Greg Filip/PPL; Illustrations: Greg Filip and Kara Thomas; Photo research: PPL Photo Agency; Photographs: Andrew Pickthall/PPL: 61, 74; Andrew Sewell: 80; Barry Pickthall/PPL: 8, 13, 15, 17, 23, 36, 42, 48, 54, 63, 79, 96, 106, 107, 110, 111, 118, 126; Bob Grieser/PPL: 116; Don Carr/103; Dreamstime.com: 1, 3, 19, 46/7, 52/3, 56/7, 70/71, 98, 112, 113, 114, 115, 130, 131; Gary Fry: 6, 9, 19, 51, 61, 133, 144; Gary-John Norman/PPL: 10, 31/32, 33/34, 97; HM Customs/PPL: 14; iStockphoto: 24-25; John Nugent: 37; Kate Pickthall/PPL: 77; Lee Sanitation/PPL: 38; Mark Pepper/PPL: 34, 45; MDL/PPL: 35; Premier Marinas/PPL: 105; RAF/PPL: 94; Riva/PPL: 11; RMA/PPL: 26; Simrad: 112, 113, 115; Tim Bishop: 41, 44, 49, 72/3, 81, 85, 86, 87, 88, 89, 90, 91, 99; WSCC/PPL: 76.

Contents

The visitors' pontoon in St Peter Port, Guernsey.

Introduction

My first foreign voyage was across the English Channel as an 18 year-old raw recruit in the annual Cowes–Dinard yacht race. *Joran*, a 36ft One-tonner had won this classic the previous year and, owned by one of Edward Heath's prime afterguard figures on his Sydney Hobart race–winning yacht *Morning Cloud*, I had joined a hot crew.

To say that I was out of my depth would be a major understatement. My previous experience had been limited to sailing dinghies. I had not been out of sight of land before, never worked in a watch system, never tried to change sails on a heaving deck at night, nor suffered from seasickness.

Deauville harbour – a favourite destination for those crossing the English Channel.

The two lighthouses guarding the harbour entrance to Belle Isle, Brittany.

Clear skies and smooth seas...but it is not always like this. Hence the need to prepare for all eventualities.

Four decades on, I have crossed the Channel many times both under power and sail, cruised the Caribbean, and rounded both the Capes of Good Hope and Horn – but never as skipper. It was only in recent times, having retired from the daily grind of reporting on sport, that my children, now grown up, pressured me to take them on their first foreign sea cruise.

Having been a guest crew all these years, I was blissfully unaware of all the responsibilities a skipper has for his crew and vessel. Preparing our 27ft yacht *Sea Jay* for an extended cruise to France proved quite an eye-opener, even for this seasoned sailor.

If the bureaucrats have their way, soon it will not be possible to just up-anchor and head wherever the wind takes you. Proposed EU immigration regulations stipulate that all vessels must file a 'flight plan' and keep authorities informed at every stage, just as if you were flying a plane. Then there are the registration and insurance stipulations; life raft, flares and radio, not to mention the small matter of qualifications: the Yachtmaster ticket and the International Certificate of Competence. The latter are not required to simply sail your own boat across the Channel for the present, but they could well be in the future.

The boat also requires a thorough check. There are spares to be carried and most importantly, the crew need to be trained in safety at sea and man overboard manoeuvres.

What if the skipper falls overboard? Is the crew capable of controlling the boat and returning to recover him or her safely? Mine would not have been. What if there is a fire onboard? Does the crew know where the extinguishers and fire blankets are, and what to do? If flames take hold, this is no time to start instructing on fire drill.

Then there are the comic catastrophes: running aground, forgetting a vital component like the spinnaker pole, overcoming electrical failure, the difficulties of cooking in a confined area, and the many uses for a bucket!

My own memories of going foreign for the first time are ones of adventure and sense of achievement. The short bout of sickness I experienced has been long forgotten. The most memorable aspects were a glorious spinnaker reach down the French coast to St Malo followed by dinner in the celebrated Duchess Anne restaurant. On our return, we cruised back through the Channel Islands, dropping anchor at Alderney for another run ashore, another memorable meal and the inevitable duty free booty.

That week re-shaped my whole life. The comradeship that bonded our crew for those overnight voyages continue to this day. I couldn't wait for the next opportunity. I traded in my chosen career for the pen and camera of a sailing journalist and have been sailing the seven seas ever since. The restaurant experience also began a life-long love of French cuisine and a penchant for restaurants with Michelin stars!

Going foreign should be fun. This book is a practical, anecdotal companion for all those sailing overseas for the first time. It simplifies the bureaucracy and prepares you for the unexpected to ensure a safe and enjoyable cruise. And anyone planning a Channel crossing should be sure to have the *Reeds Nautical Almanac* and the *Adlard Coles Nautical Logbook* onboard.

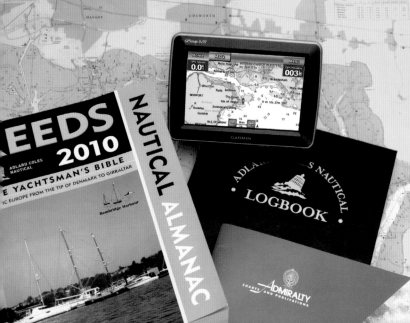

Companion books to keep on the shelf.

Paperwork

What paperwork do I need to carry?

Ship's papers

These must all be original documents (photocopies are not acceptable), and comprise:

Registration document: This is compulsory if you intend to take a non-commercial pleasure craft outside UK territorial waters. This applies both to boats that are sailed or driven to a foreign port, or trailered on the road by train or ferry.

Customs officers are now in the front line to apprehend illegal immigrants.

Proof of ownership: A bill of sale is required for vessels registered on the UK Small Ships Register (SSR) because this register only indicates the vessel's nationality, and not ownership of the vessel. If the owner is not onboard, the skipper is required to carry a letter authorising use of the vessel to prove that the loan is not an illegal charter arrangement.

Proof of VAT status: Residents of the EU can only use vessels within Community waters if VAT has been paid or 'deemed' to have been paid. Proof of the VAT status of a vessel is not part of the ship's papers, so it is required in order to prove that the boat

Keep all your paperwork in order – it could be expensive if you can't show it when asked by Customs officials at either end of the voyage.

is entitled to free movement throughout the EU. If documentary evidence is not readily available in the form of a receipted invoice or similar, customs officials have the power to impound your boat, so be warned.

Recreational Craft Compliant: If your vessel was built or imported into the EU, including Iceland, Liechtenstein, Norway and Switzerland after 16th June 1998, you are required to carry proof that your boat is Recreational Craft Directing (RCD) Compliant. This requirement is satisfied by the Builder's CE mark, shown on the manufacturer's plate, which certifies that a product has met EU consumer safety, health and environmental requirements.

Ship Radio Licence: Under the International Radio Regulations, vessels with any kind of radio transmitter, even a hand-held VHF, must have a licence. Ofcom issues the licence in the UK, and applications can be made online at www.ofcom.org.uk. The licence details the equipment onboard, and covers:

- Fixed or portable VHF or VHF/DSC radio
- MF/HF radio equipment
- AIS transponder
- Emergency Position Indicating Radio Beacon (EPIRB)
- Personal Locator Beacon (PLB)
- Radar
- Satellite communications
- Search and Rescue Transponder (SART)
- Ship Earth Station (SES) equipment

Check if your set has an Active Radar Target Enhancer or is ATIS capable, since these are not available to select on the list of licensable equipment and you need to request a variation to your Ship Radio Licence. The licence has to be updated whenever changes are made to the equipment onboard.

Call signs and Maritime Mobile Service Identity (MMSI) numbers are allocated when the first application is made. This call sign remains valid for the lifetime of the vessel regardless of changes in ownership or name, unless the boat is sold outside the UK.

Are you fully licensed to use a marine radio?
Does your vessel have an MMSI number?

MMSI numbers are only issued when Digital Selective Calling (DSC) and/or Ship Earth Station (SES) equipment is fitted.

Remember that EPIRBs must be registered both on the Ship Radio Licence and with the MCA EPIRB Registry to ensure that all Maritime Rescue Co-ordination Centres (MRCC) have the necessary information should your EPIRB be activated.

European inland waterways: Under the Regional Arrangement Concerning the Radiotelephone Service on Inland Waterways (RAINWAT), all vessels navigating the inland waterways of central Europe must be equipped with a VHF radio with an active ATIS transmission facility. An ATIS number is issued by Ofcom as a Notice of Variation to the Ship Radio Licence. For the moment, Ofcom does this manually, and applicants must allow up to a month for details of the vessel to be activated by the European regulator, the Belgian Institute for Post and Telecommunications (BIPT).

Ofcom provides answers to FAQs about ATIS and RAINWAT on their website, www.ofcom.org.uk. It also explains how to request the Notice of Variation to your Ship Radio Licence and obtain the ATIS number for your vessel. You must also carry a copy of the Basel Arrangement governing ATIS onboard. This can be downloaded from the RAINWAT website, www.rainwat.bipt.be

Hand-held radio: The Ship Portable Radio Licence is only valid in UK waters. Licencees voyaging within RAINWAT countries must apply for a full Ship Radio Licence. If your vessel does not have an MMSI number, then you can obtain one by e-mailing licensingcentre@ofcom.org.uk

Digital Selective Calling (DSC) VHF radio transmitters are not yet mandatory aboard small pleasure craft in UK waters, but new small craft VHF sets are now Global Maritime Distress Safety System (GMDSS) compatible, though with some, the DSC element has to be purchased separately. DSC is a tone signalling system similar to the tone dialling on your phone, operating on VHF Channel 70. It has the ability to include other information such as the vessel's identification number, the purpose of the call, your position, the channel you want to speak on – and when necessary, the nature of distress.

All vessels navigating Europe's inland waterways must be equipped with a black water holding tank or have its toilet system sealed shut.

The distress message is repeated automatically every 4 minutes until acknowledged either by a Coastguard station or ship within radio range.

The minimum standard for small craft DSC-equipped radios for fixed use in Europe is EN 301 025. Check that the equipment is marked in accordance with the EU Radio and Telecommunications Terminal Equipment (R&TTE).

Maritime Radio Operator's Certificate: A VHF radio may be used by anyone in emergency situations, but can only be used for general transmissions by a licensed operator or person under the direct supervision of someone with a Maritime Radio Operator's Certificate.

The Short Range Certificate (SRC) covering the use of VHF/DSC equipment is the common operator's certificate for cruising vessels. You must attend a day-long course at a sailing school or club to gain the certificate.

A Long Range Certificate (LRC) is required for MF, HF and satellite communications equipment. The LRC is administered by the Association of Marine Electronic and Radio Colleges (AMERC). Courses range from 3–4 days and include an examination, which you must pass to gain the certificate.

Marine Insurance: This is mandatory in most European countries. Some specify minimum levels of third party cover and others require a translation, which your insurer should provide.

It is essential to check the policy for territorial limits since you may need to extend the limited cruising range stipulated. It makes good sense to inform the insurer of your yacht anyway and check that you are fully covered for all eventualities. This cover can often be extended to include personal health and repatriation cover. Beware of the standard travel insurance plans bought online or at airports, since some set restrictions on boating.

All crew should also carry a European Health Insurance Card (EHIC), the passport to free or reduced-cost emergency medical treatment within the European Economic Area (EEA) and Switzerland.

These can be applied for online at www.ehic.org

The EHIC is no substitute for medical or travel insurance because it does not cover medical repatriation, ongoing medical treatment, or treatment of a non-urgent nature. Nor is it valid in the Channel Islands where visitors are now required to pay for all medical treatment.

Personal papers

Passport: Each crew member must carry a passport. The crew may also require visas if you intend to cruise outside EU waters. Check well ahead of time because visas can take several days to get. If you have a non-EU citizen onboard, they will need to clear through immigration each time you cross from one country to another, even if the vessel is not required to clear customs.

International Certificate of Competence (ICC): Whilst it is not (yet) a requirement for UK skippers of pleasure craft below 24m (78.74ft) or 80 tonnes to have a certificate of competence or licence, this is not the same in all EU countries. The requirements vary from country to country so you need to check out what is required in advance. You can do this through the country's National Sailing Authority or embassy.

If you do not hold a Yachtmaster certificate and are chartering a vessel or cruising in Northern Europe, a letter from a Flag Officer or Club Secretary outlining your experience and competence may suffice. However, skippers of UK flagged vessels are required to hold an ICC when cruising the inland waterways of Europe and inland and coastal waters of Mediterranean countries. Certainly, anyone planning to charter abroad should ask the charter company for details of the certification they require to meet local laws and insurance requirements.

The ICC is NOT a qualification. It is simply documentary assurance from one government to another that the holder meets locally accepted levels of competence. It allows UK citizens and residents to navigate pleasure craft in the waters of participating states without the need to comply with national transport laws, in particular, compulsory certification requirements.

European inland waterways: In addition to holding an ICC, you must also learn the Code Européen des Voies de la Navigation I (CEVNI) which governs navigation on the interconnected Europe waterways. You will need to pass a short multiple-choice exam at a recognised sailing school.

How do I apply for an ICC or CEVNI?

The Royal Yachting Association (RYA) is the UK issuing authority for the ICC and CEVNI endorsement. To prove your competence to gain an ICC you must have attained an RYA practical training certificate in one of the following categories:

- Radio Operator's Certificate, GMDSS Short Range Certificate or higher grade of marine radio certificate.

- First aid certificate. First aid qualifications held by Police, Fire and Armed Services are also acceptable.

Remember that the ICC is valid only for the type of vessel and level that you passed your competence test on. The minimum age is 16.

e-Borders – what new EU legislation could mean to you

The aim of new e-Borders legislation is to collect and analyse information about everyone intending to travel to or from the United Kingdom before they leave in order to provide the Security Services with a comprehensive record of everyone crossing UK borders.

The legislation, requiring all cruising folk to file the equivalent of a 'flight plan' listing crew details and intended destination, every time you set out from your marina berth or mooring, was due to come into force at the end of 2010.

However, a government report questioned the legality of the e-Borders programme as it would cut across the overriding principle of EU residents having the right to travel freely within the entire EU. So the current leaky border controls will continue until someone comes up with a brighter plan.

However, you still need to have all your vessel and crew paperwork in order, even though the sole interest for 9 out of 10 harbour officials remains focused on how you are going to pay for the berthing facilities.

Are you certified? The bureaucracy and paperwork may drive some of us up the wall, but an International Certificate of Competence, radio licence and first aid certificate are not only essential, but make sense.

Course certificate requirement	ICC may be issued for				
	Power		Sail	Inland Waters CEVNI test required	Coastal waters
	up to 10m	up to 24m	up to 24m		
National Powerboat Certificate (non tidal) **Level 2 or above**	✓			✓	
National Powerboat Certificate (tidal) **Level 2 or above**	✓			✓	✓
Helmsman's Course Completion Certificate		✓		✓	✓
Inland Waterways Helmsman Certificate		✓		✓	✓
Day Skipper Practical Course Completion Certificate (Power)		✓		✓	✓
Day Skipper Practical Course Completion Certificate (Sail)	✓		✓	✓	✓
Coastal Skipper Practical Course Completion Certificate (Power)		✓		✓	✓
Coastal Skipper Practical Course Completion Certificate (Sail)	✓		✓	✓	✓

Course certificate requirement	ICC may be issued for					
	Power		Sail	Inland Waters CEVNI test required	Coastal waters	Personal water-craft
	up to 10m	up to 24m	up to 24m			
MCA Deck Officer Certificate of Competence (any grade)		✓		✓	✓	
RN, Army or RAF Bridge Watchkeeping Certificate	✓		✓	✓	✓	
MCA or Local Authority Boatman's Licence		✓		✓	✓	
MCA Boatmaster Certificate		✓		✓	✓	
RYA Dinghy Instructor and National Powerboat Certificate Level 2 or higher		✓		✓	✓	
Personal Watercraft Proficiency Certificate		✓		✓	✓	
Coastal Skipper Practical Course Completion Certificate (Power)	✓		✓	✓	✓	
Coastal Skipper Practical Course Completion Certificate (Sail)					✓	✓

Is the boat up to scratch? Have you the tools and spares onboard to cover any eventualities?

3 The boat

Power or sail, never set out on an extended voyage without giving the vessel a thorough check, and always carry a comprehensive range of spares and tools in the event of breakdown. On the Continent, spares are not always so easy to buy off the shelf, and having the right fuel filter or engine belt stored onboard could well save your holiday.

The sea is a harsh environment and salt water a particularly corrosive element. Engines are invariably the heartbeat of your boat, for even if you expect to rely on sail, they charge the batteries and provide the power to get you into port. If they stop, then so do you, so treat them like a best friend by checking them over before and after each voyage.

	Routine checks
1	Check oil levels in engine and gearbox
2	Check fresh water coolant levels
3	Check seawater inlet and strainer for debris
4	Check hydraulic oil levels
5	Check belt tension and wear
6	Check fuel filters for water and particles
7	Keep fuel tanks topped up to minimise condensation
8	Inspect the engine for oil and water leaks before and after a passage
9	Keep the engine bay clean. Oil-absorbing pads left in the bilges will contain drips
10	Check piping for signs of perishing or splits
11	Check sacrificial anodes and replace when necessary
12	Follow manufacturer's recommendations for servicing

Safety equipment

Safety at sea covers everything from basic equipment, spares and tools to first aid. Here is a thorough checklist for motor and sailing vessels.

Safety equipment checklist	Motor	Sail
■ Anchor and chain (2)	✓	✓
■ Bilge pumps (2 – manual and electric)	✓	✓
■ Boat hook	✓	✓
■ Bosun's chair		✓
■ Buckets (2) with lanyards	✓	✓
■ Compass	✓	✓
■ Dan buoy attached to lifebuoy		✓
■ Distress flares – MCA approved Offshore flare pack containing:	✓	✓
• 2 orange smoke hand flares	✓	✓
• 2 white hand flares	✓	✓
• 4 red parachute rockets	✓	✓
• 6 red hand flares	✓	✓
■ Jack stays		✓
■ Lifebuoy with light, whistle and drogue attached	✓	✓
■ Lifejacket with a crotch strap, whistle, and light for each crewmember	✓	✓
■ Liferaft	✓	✓
■ Radar reflector	✓	✓

Safety equipment checklist, cont.	Motor	Sail
■ Sail ties		✓
■ Search & Rescue Transponder (SART)	✓	✓
■ Spare lines	✓	✓
■ Spare fuel and water (25 litres of each)	✓	✓
■ Trisail or a mainsail with 3 reefing points, and storm jib		✓
■ Washboards		✓
■ Fire extinguishers in each cabin	✓	✓
■ Fire extinguisher (remote controlled) in engine compartment	✓	✓
■ Fire blanket in galley	✓	✓
■ Torch/search light	✓	✓
■ Softwood spherical bung taped to each skin fitting	✓	✓

Tool kit	Motor	Sail
■ Adjustable wrench	✓	✓
■ Bolt croppers		✓
■ Cable ties	✓	✓
■ Centre punch	✓	✓
■ Duck tape	✓	✓
■ Electrical crimping tool + connectors	✓	✓
■ Electrical tape	✓	✓
■ Emery cloth or boards	✓	✓
■ Epoxy rapid cement	✓	✓
■ Gasket cement	✓	✓
■ Hammer	✓	✓
■ Hand drill	✓	✓
■ Hose clips	✓	✓
■ Junior hacksaw	✓	✓
■ Long nose pliers	✓	✓
■ Mole grips	✓	✓
■ Plastic piping	✓	✓
■ Round file	✓	✓
■ Rubber mallet	✓	✓
■ Set of allen keys	✓	✓
■ Set of drill bits	✓	✓
■ Set of flat head screwdrivers	✓	✓

Tool kit, cont.	Motor	Sail
■ Set of Phillips screwdrivers	✓	✓
■ Set of spanners	✓	✓
■ Socket set	✓	✓
■ Spare batteries	✓	✓
■ Spare bulbs and fuses	✓	✓
■ Stanley knife	✓	✓
■ Tape measure	✓	✓
■ Waterproof grease	✓	✓
■ Wire brush	✓	✓

Sail repair kit	Motor	Sail
■ Dacron sail repair tape		✓
■ Fid		✓
■ Mousing wire		✓
■ Needles and thread		✓
■ Sailmaker's palm		✓
■ Spare shackles		✓
■ Whipping twine		✓

Nav station checklist	Motor	Sail
Admiralty list of lights	✓	✓
Admiralty radio signals	✓	✓
Almanac	✓	✓
Back-up radio receiver (wind-up)	✓	✓
Barometer	✓	✓
Binoculars	✓	✓
Boat data file	✓	✓
Breton plotter	✓	✓
Calculator	✓	✓
Charts for the region (up to date)	✓	✓
Clock	✓	✓
Dividers	✓	✓
Echo sounder	✓	✓
Emergency torch (wind-up)	✓	✓
Eraser	✓	✓
GPS	✓	✓
Hand-held VHF with charger	✓	✓
Hand-bearing compass	✓	✓
Lead line	✓	✓
Log book	✓	✓
Long wave receiver (for forecasts)	✓	✓

Nav station checklist, cont.	Motor	Sail
■ Mobile phone and charger	✓	✓
■ Parallel rule or plotter	✓	✓
■ Pencils and sharpener	✓	✓
■ Pilot books	✓	✓
■ Portable VHF, charger and emergency aerial	✓	✓
■ Symbols and abbreviations chart	✓	✓
■ Tidal atlas	✓	✓
■ Torch	✓	✓

Grab bag checklist	Motor	Sail
■ Flares	✓	✓
■ Food	✓	✓
■ Portable VHF	✓	✓
■ Water	✓	✓

Engine spares checklist	Motor	Sail
■ Spare alternator belt	✓	✓
■ Spare engine oil filters	✓	✓
■ Spare fuel filters	✓	✓
■ Spare water pump filter	✓	✓
■ Spare water pump belt	✓	✓
■ Spare water pump impeller	✓	✓

4 Hull checks

How clean is your hull? A weedy or barnacle-encrusted bottom will not only knock a few knots off your speed, but add considerably to the fuel bill at the end of the holiday!

Powerboats invariably have to be lifted out to be jet washed in order to protect their props and steering, but owners of sailing yachts can take the more cost-effective option of spending a tide either up on a hard, or tied against scrubbing piles. Whichever, the time and cost spent cleaning off the hull, checking the state of sacrificial anodes, prop shafts, rudders and bow thrusters will not only save on the pocket, but give you considerable peace of mind.

Photo opposite and below. Having the hull cleaned will not only increase speed and fuel efficiency, but the process gives you an opportunity to give the hull a thorough check.

Cleaning tips

■ Plan the lift-out at least a week before your intended passage to give you time to rectify unforeseen problems.

■ Check for wear in the prop shaft thrust bearings and replace if necessary.

■ Check the props for damage. Propellers operate under high pressure, so any nicks have a disproportionate effect on their efficiency. If damage is superficial, it may be possible to smooth the trailing edge with a file. Anything more though, and replacement is the only option.

■ Check the rudders for bearing wear, together with the linkages or hydraulic cables for damage.

Electronics check

Run a check on navigation lights, and have a spare battery-powered set ready to hand. The navigation lights on *Sea Jay* failed once during the dead of night when a wire was shaken loose while bashing through heavy head seas. We were left totally in the dark and I have carried a spare set of lights ever since. These can be bound with duck tape to the lifelines and pushpit with minutes and the batteries last for at least two nights at sea.

It is a good idea to check through all the electronics and to swing the compass. GPS-linked chart plotters are wonderful aids, but if the compass has not been calibrated, you could find yourself well off your intended landfall when crossing the Channel or North Sea.

Sailing yachts should always undergo a thorough safety check on rig, sails, reefing systems and

Has the compass been swung? It could be giving a false heading.

Can your vessel take the ground? If so, then there are plenty of free moorings to be found, particularly on Brittany beaches. You can always carry sea legs if she can't stand on her keel.

deck hardware. If the yacht is well maintained, then a visual check for halyard chafe will uncover potential problems here but also look at the lines controlling furling and reefing systems. If the vessel has not been kept up to scratch, a more thorough check for hairline cracks in the spars and fittings is essential.

Other checks: Look over the sails for any telltale signs of broken stitching or chafe, especially where the cloth can rub against the spreaders or radar dome. A stitch in time…will save a lot of bother later!

Deck gear and winches should all be given a good wash with fresh soapy water to rid them of salt residue. It's often a good idea to lift off the winch barrels and apply a little grease to the pawls. It is far easier to do this on the dock than have a winch go down during a passage and try to repair it on the high seas.

If you intend to head for the high tidal rise and falls found around the Brittany coast and Channel Islands and your vessel is not capable of standing the ground, consider taking sea legs. They will allow you to take the ground in sheltered coves and provide a second option if the marina is full.

Discharging black water waste at a marina pump-out station. This is the ecological way to deal with toilet waste, but rules vary across the EU and Baltic states. Only on inland waters across the EU is the pumping of raw sewage banned. If you don't have a black water waste system onboard, the heads must be sealed shut.

Waste disposal

A million birds and 100,000 marine mammals die around the world each year from entanglement or ingestion of plastics. In Britain, harbour authorities spend on average £26,000 each year removing debris from the water and clearing fouled props. Rubbish takes a surprisingly long time to degrade. A cigarette butt takes 5 years, if birds don't eat them first. A tin can will survive 50 years under water, an aluminium can twice that time, and glass bottles take up to a 1,000 years to turn back to sand.

The simple answer is not to drop anything over the side. If you happen to do so by accident, then practice your man overboard drill to retrieve it! You have only to experience the costly problem of having a plastic bag blocking the engine inlet once to become a recycling convert.

Here are some simple tips:

- Remove excess packaging before carrying it onboard and recycle at home.
- Prevent plastic bags, food and drink cans and loose items from blowing overboard.
- Use recycling facilities at marinas, clubs and harbour authorities.

Rules for discharging holding tanks

The EU might have strict rules governing such ludicrous things as the size and shape of bananas, and force fishermen to throw back dead fish to stay within their quotas, but it is remarkably sanguine when it comes to controlling pollution.

Regulations regarding the discharge of sewage are gradually increasing, but as yet there is no international convention requiring private pleasure craft to fit a holding tank. For the present, it is down to each country to control the discharge of sewage as it sees fit. That means the rules vary from one state to another. Black water is toilet waste ie waste that will often contain harmful bacteria and viruses. Grey water is bilge water and discharge from sinks and wash basins.

Netherlands

Since early 2009 it has been prohibited to discharge black water from all pleasure boats on inland waterways, lakes, the Waddensea and territorial waters. Existing pleasure boats must either have holding tanks, dry or chemical toilets fitted, or boaters could choose simply not to use their toilets.

France

The French have always taken a very laid back attitude to toilets. In principle it is forbidden to flush toilets into canals and rivers, but as pump-out facilities are few and far between, discreet overboard discharging continues to be tolerated on inland and coastal waters.

The Baltic countries of **Denmark, Estonia, Finland, Germany, Latvia, Lithuania, Poland, Russia and Sweden** are all signatories to the HELCOM Convention on the protection of the marine environment of the Baltic Sea Area, but some have yet to implement the rules nationally. Thus, the ban on discharging sewage is not yet law across the whole region.

Finland is one country where the the discharge of untreated sewage is prohibited within 12 nautical miles of the coast.

In Denmark, boats built before 1 January 1980 do not have to have a holding tank and can discharge sewage when 2 nautical miles from the shore. Boats built before 1 January 2000 and are either less than 10.5m LOA or have a maximum beam of less than 2.8m, do not have to have a holding tank and can also discharge sewage when outside the 2 nautical mile limit. Boats built after 1 January 2000 must have a holding tank that can be emptied through a deck fitting.

Inland Waterways

The rules vary from country to country, but like all toiletry issues, the answer is basic. If you don't want to fish, swim or float in sewage, keep it tanked.

Rules and regulations regarding toilet waste vary from country to country, but if you don't want to fish, swim or float in sewage, keep it tanked.

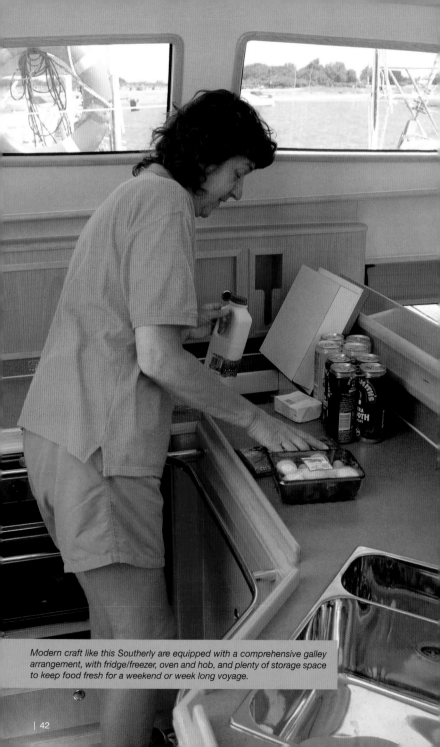

Modern craft like this Southerly are equipped with a comprehensive galley arrangement, with fridge/freezer, oven and hob, and plenty of storage space to keep food fresh for a weekend or week long voyage.

Provisioning

Preparing for a 2–5 day passage

Much of the food for a weekend trip or even a 5-day passage can be prepared at home and stored onboard as pre-cooked meals in the fridge or freezer and served cold or simply reheated.

Simple fare is often best. A cold, hungry crew really appreciate hot stews, shepherd's pie, and lasagne, which can all be prepared ahead of time. These can easily be supplemented with simple things like tins of good soup – great for a heart warming mid-watch snack – or pasta and bottled or packaged sauces.

At times when it is too rough to cook on a stove, there are ready made boil-in-the-bag meals to fall back on. These sealed packets are either dropped into a pot of boiling water or the freeze-dried contents mixed with hot water from a vacuum flask. These packet foods last for years and are good stand-bys to have onboard.

High protein foods are key: Stock up on bread, cereals, cheese, eggs, fish, jams, meat and milk, complimented with vegetables like beans and peas.

Carry a minimum of 2 litres of water per person per day, which can be supplemented with glucose or barley water soft drinks. We always have a pump action vacuum flask filled with hot water on the go all night for crew to make themselves cups of tea, coffee or hot chocolate through the colder watches. Nutritional cereal bars, chocolate bars and biscuits also go down well.

A pressure cooker not only saves gas, but can be used to cook the complete meal...and keep it hot for the next watch. The push button vacuum flask tied in place is another must have.

Fresh food

Fresh produce, chosen with care can also remain edible for long periods if stored correctly. Eggs for instance, bought straight from the farm, can last for 6 weeks or more, even when sailing in the Tropics. Lettuces too will last well if roots are retained and the plants are stored in open boxes on a mattress of damp paper or cotton wool. These and any other vegetables need to be washed in fresh water before being carried onboard, and stored preferably in nets strung across the galley, rather than polythene bags which promote sweating and early rot.

One labour-saving device is a pressure cooker, especially if it has trays stacked inside to separate the food. They are a great gas saver, as meals take less time to cook than in open pans, and it can also be used to boil water safely. Another benefit is that it keeps the meal hot between watches without the need to reheat.

Keep a plan of where everything is stored. Otherwise meals can become something of a Russian roulette.

Storage

Keep a plan of where everything is stored and tick off the list as stocks are consumed. If you can code everything, so much the better because then everyone onboard will be able to find what they are looking for easily.

Canned food should always be stored as close to the centre of buoyancy as possible so that it has least effect on trim, but remember to keep cans well away from the compass. The same applies to the beer!

Seasickness remedies

If there are seasickness sufferers onboard, refrain from fry-ups – the smell alone can turn stomachs! Fizzy water can help an upset tummy and dry, plain crackers are a good starter to nibble on once the sickness has subsided.

Product	Shelf life	Once opened consume within
CEREALS		
Oats – packet	6 months	re-seal
Breakfast cereals – individual packs	6 months	1 day
SOUPS		
Soups – pre-prepared sachet	18 months	1 day
Soups – powders	18 months	1 week
PRE-PREPARED VEGETABLES		
Chopped tomatoes – Tetra pack	2 years	1 day
Tomato puree – tube	2 years	3 weeks
Dried mushrooms – packet	18 months	2 days
Dried tomatoes – packet	18 months	2 days
Dried onions – packet	18 months	2 days
Garlic puree – tube	2 years	3 weeks
Sweet corn – tin	30 months	2 days
Freeze dried peas – packet	2 years	1 month
SAUCES		
Tomato sauce – sachet	18 months	2 days
Stir-fry sauce – sachet	2 years	2 days
Cheese sauce granules – cardboard can	1 year	re-seal
Gravy granules – cardboard can	1 year	re-seal
CHILD PACIFIERS		
Dried fruits – sachet	1 year	4 weeks

Product	Shelf life	Once opened consume within
CARBOHYDRATES		
Dried pasta – packet	2 years	re-seal
Pre-cooked rice – sachet	2 years	2 days
Tuscan bean mix – packet	1 year	1 day
Potato mash – packet	2 years	1 day
MEAT AND FISH		
Anchovies, mackerel, sardines, salmon, tuna – tinned	3 years	2 days
Chorizo sausage, cured ham – packet	3 months	2 days
Beef/chicken stew – tin cans	3 years	2 days
PUDDINGS		
Custard – Tetra pack	2 years	3 days
Fruit fillings – tin cans	30 months	3 days
Crumble mix – sachet	2 years	1 week
Pancake mix – plastic container/sachet	2 years	3 days
BASICS		
Spreadable butter/margarine – tub	3 months	1 month
Olive oil – spray	30 months	3 months
Long life cream – plastic cans	6 months	3 days
Long life milk – Tetra pack	6 months	3 days
Cream crackers	6 months	1 day

The pretty French port of Honfleur, a favourite destination on the Seine estuary.

6 Planning the voyage

Crossing the English Channel or North Sea for the first time can be quite an adventure for all the crew, so get them involved at an early stage in the planning, and share out the responsibilities. There is something for everyone to do. At the start of a recent Atlantic Rally for Cruisers, I was impressed to find one 6-year-old had been given the task of drawing up the rules onboard. Writ largest among the amusing list of dos and don'ts were the words 'NO SMOKING' for the grown-ups to take note of.

The best time to make an open sea crossing from the UK is in June when the days are longest and the weather is often at its best, although GPS and chart plotters have taken all the guesswork out of estimating night time plots, or the need to catch the flash of a lighthouse before dawn, extending the 'first time' window from Easter to September.

Sharing responsibilities. Even the youngest members of the crew can have a role to play.

Something to look forward to! Fresh fish, baguettes, cheese, paté and local wines straight from the dockside market await your arrival in most ports on the Continent.

Planning

The first task is to agree a destination and work backwards. For those on the South Coast, the simplest is a straight course south, crossing the traffic separation zones at right angles, and arrive at your French port in daylight. If you are setting out from anywhere other than the eastern end of the Channel, this will invariably mean leaving at night, because it is far better to navigate waters you know in darkness, than arrive at night in areas you don't.

By the end of 2010, it may be necessary in European waters at least, to file a crew list and route plan each time you set out to sea, so do this ahead of time and make sure that you carry passport/ID and sailing/radio qualification certificates along with insurance documents and the ship's registration and VAT papers. And remember to update the details online if weather or circumstance forces you to change your route.

What destination?
Decide on a final destination and ETA that matches tidal access, and then work back to select rendezvous or refuelling points, and review danger areas and tidal gates. You also need to select one or more refuge ports in the event of adverse weather or other eventualities.

The entrance to Ploumanach in Northern Brittany is not the easiest of harbours to enter. Make a detailed pilotage plan listing landmarks and markers, whatever your route.

Destination port

- High and low water times
- Depth restrictions over entrance bar or harbour sill
- Check shipping movements
- Local dangers – rocks, shallows and wrecks etc
- Marina or harbour radio channel and telephone numbers
- Check anchorage
- Ground type
- Ferry times
- Pre-book marina berth
- List of destinations and alternative ports
- Distances between ports or waypoints
- Estimate fuel consumption and add 20% safety margin
- Estimate passage time between points taking account of tidal stream

Plot

- Danger areas
- Landmarks
- Traffic separation schemes
- Waypoints

Food

- Plan menus with good nutritional value
- Prepare food ahead of time
- Drinks: Minimum of 2 litres of water per person per day
- Have flasks ready with hot drinks or soup for the night watch

Weather

- Tune in to weather forecasts 2–3 days before voyage
- Monitor approaching depressions

Once onboard

- Check fuel and oil levels
- Check latest weather forecast
- Crew safety briefing
- Decide go or no-go
- Enter waypoints in GPS course plotter

During passage

- Check fuel consumption
- Crew – keep them informed and involved
- Check weather and sea state

What to carry onboard

- *Reeds Nautical Almanac* ■ *Adlard Coles Nautical Log Book*
- Charts of cruising area (up to date)
- Chart plotter
- Cruising guide and pilot books
- Dividers
- Eraser
- Pencils
- Tidal atlas

Fall back plan

- Crew issues
- Delays
- Tidal gates
- Weather change

Wind against tide situations faced by this crew reaching with the stream but facing short, sharp seas from the opposing wind in the Great Russel Channel off Herm, can be avoided by timing your passage to coincide with slack water. It will also be easier to spot the lobster pot markers that are often submerged by the fast-running stream.

Passage plan

Planning the passage ahead of time takes a lot of the headache and stress away from making the voyage. The passage plan should cover the distance between safe water outside your point of departure and safe water outside your destination.

Waypoints

These are the corners of your voyage around headlands, islands and buoys. If you do pick hard points on the chart, keep a wary eye open for them. There have been too many cases of vessels hitting them when running on GPS guided autopilots!

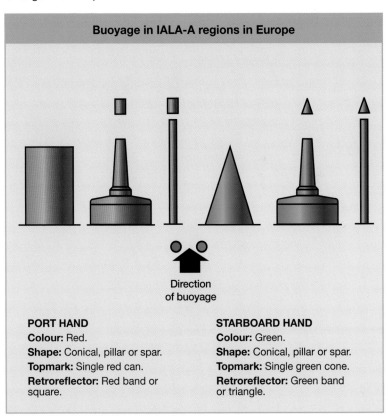

Buoyage in IALA-A regions in Europe

Direction
of buoyage

PORT HAND
Colour: Red.
Shape: Conical, pillar or spar.
Topmark: Single red can.
Retroreflector: Red band or square.

STARBOARD HAND
Colour: Green.
Shape: Conical, pillar or spar.
Topmark: Single green cone.
Retroreflector: Green band or triangle.

LIGHTS, when fitted, may have any rhythm other than composite group flashing (2+ l) used on modified lateral marks indicating a preferred channel. Examples are:

Q.G	Continuous-quick light	Q.R
Fl.G	Single-flashing light	Fl.R
LFl.G	Long-flashing light	LFl.R
Fl(2)G	Group-flashing light	Fl(2)R

Red or green lights are frequently used for minor shore lights, such as those marking pier heads and the extremities of jetties.

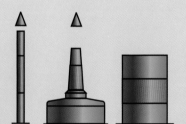 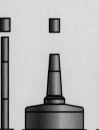

Direction
of buoyage

*Composite group
flashing (2+ l) light*

Fl (2+1)G   Fl(2+1)R

Preferred channel to port
Colour: Green with one broad red band.
Shape: Conical, pillar or spar.
Topmark (when fitted): Single green cone point upward.
Retroreflector: Green band or triangle.

Preferred channel to starboard
Colour: Red with one broad green band.
Shape: Conical, pillar or spar.
Topmark (when fitted): Single red can.
Retroreflector: Red band or square.

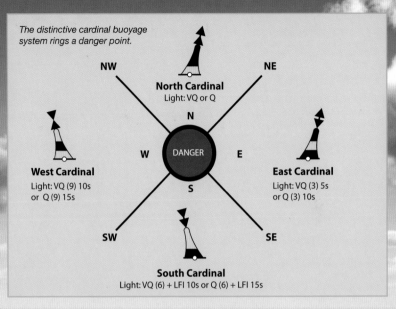

The distinctive cardinal buoyage system rings a danger point.

NW

North Cardinal
Light: VQ or Q

NE

W

DANGER

N

E

S

West Cardinal
Light: VQ (9) 10s
or Q (9) 15s

East Cardinal
Light: VQ (3) 5s
or Q (3) 10s

SW

SE

South Cardinal
Light: VQ (6) + LFl 10s or Q (6) + LFl 15s

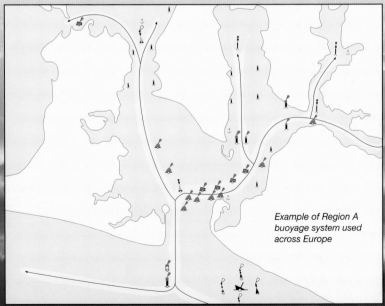

Example of Region A buoyage system used across Europe

Alternative ports

Always plan havens to divert to in the event of adverse weather, mechanical problems or illness. Include the course and tidal changes as well as a pilotage plan for the entrance in your overall plan, and you won't be caught short at a difficult time.

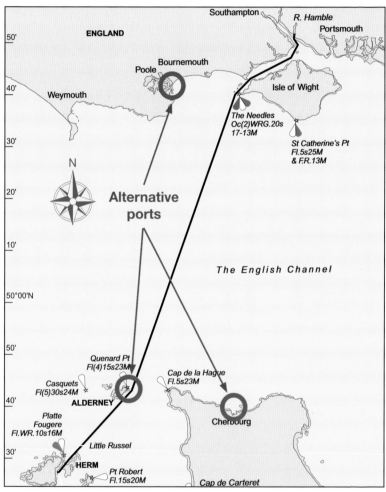

Alternative ports: If you are planning a voyage to the Channel Islands, then Poole and Cherbourg, which have all-tide, all-weather access, are the best refuge ports. If you miss the tidal gate at Alderney, then Braye harbour is the best option to wait for the tide.

Pilotage plan

This is the detailed plan for entering or leaving a harbour to provide an aide-memoire to visual points at the entrance. It should be drawn on a detailed chart and include:

- Start point
- Finish point
- Distance info
- Course info
- Tidal information
- Buoys and landmarks to port and starboard

The start and finish points must be easily identifiable by eye or radar and are preferably lit so that they can be identified at night. (See circled items on chart below).

Draw your desired track on the chart and annotate everything you are likely to see to port on the left side of the line, and anything of note to starboard, on the right side. Other information, such as distances, goes in the middle.

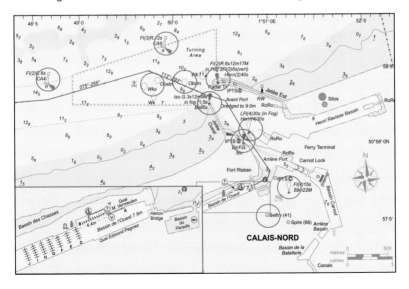

This is the pilotage plan we drew up to enter St Vaast-la-Hougue using the excellent information available in the *Reeds Nautical Almanac*.

High Water: 13:35 4.9m. **Low Water:** 20:35 2.9m
- Depth restrictions over entrance bar NONE

Harbour sill: 2.5m
- Shipping movements: Amphibious ferry from slipway north of lock gates to Ile de Tatihou

Local dangers: rocks, shallows and wrecks etc.

Marina radio: Channel 9

Telephone: +33 (0)2 336100

Waypoint: Le Gravendest south cardinal buoy 49°35'.17N 01°15'. 41W (6 quick flashes at 15 second intervals.) Round to the south

Steer: 310°M for 1.3 miles to end of harbour wall
- Stay in white sector of Grande Jetée lighthouse sited on the end of wall (2 occulting flashes at 6 second intervals) – conspicuous white tower with red top
- Pass La Dent south cardinal (unlit) to port
- Beware moored vessels to port
- Pass east cardinal buoy to starboard
- Pass east cardinal mark to starboard
- 1.3 miles: Pass lighthouse to starboard. Fort Ile de Tatihou to starboard
- Turn to port (250°M) and head for Red and Green port entrance lights marking the lock gates in north west corner of harbour
- Gate opens between HW – 2 ¼hrs and HW +3 ½hrs
- Pass through lock
- Visitor berths on B and C pontoons directly to starboard after passing through lock

Before arrival:
- Call ahead to marina or harbour office
- Call Customs/Immigration
- Raise courtesy/Q flags
- Locate mooring, berth or anchorage
- Complete log and documentation

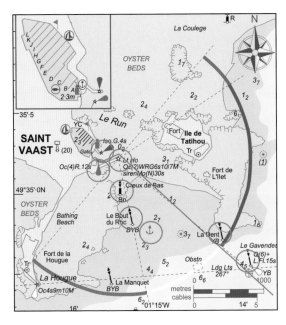

Detailed chart of St Vaast in Reeds Nautical Almanac provides all the information required to produce a detailed pilotage plan.

Arriving at the open lock gate entry to the marina in St Vaast la Hougue. The harbour office is to the right and visitors' berths immediately after.

Tidal steam – time it to work for you, rather than against you

The tidal stream is important, particularly for sailing vessels. Averaging 5 knots over the 60 miles from the Needles to Cherbourg for instance, will take 12 hours, so the changes in tidal stream east and west effectively negate each other. This is one occasion when you follow a compass course rather than what the GPS is suggesting. The stream will push you first one way away from the rhumb line, but then bring you back on track when the tide turns. On longer routes, you simply total up the east and west going tides and subtract the smaller figure from the larger one. The result is your net tidal vector, which you draw on the chart to calculate the course to steer.

If you add a mile or two up-tide of your destination port, so much the better because it is always easier to run with a fair tide under you than claw back up-tide, especially when the wind is blowing in the opposite direction.

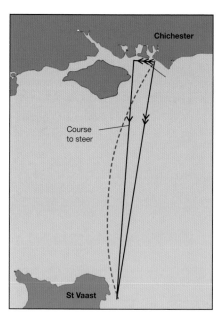

Calculate the net tidal effect east or west and follow the mean compass course. This will produce a shorter course than following directions from the chart plotter.

But even if the plan has the Dutch coast or Channel Islands as a final destination, there are tidal wheezes to take advantage of. Three tidal gates at Selsey Bill, Beachy Head and Dungeness form a tidal sequence that allow vessels to ride the progressive east going tide all the way from the East Solent to Dover. Based on a mean boat speed of 5 knots (7 knots over the ground), you can use the eddy running along the north shore from the Hamble and transit the Looe Channel at slack water (HW Dover +0500). You will then pass Beachy Head at HW Dover – 0100, Dungeness at HW Dover +0300 and reach Dover at +0530, facing only the first half hour of ebb tide.

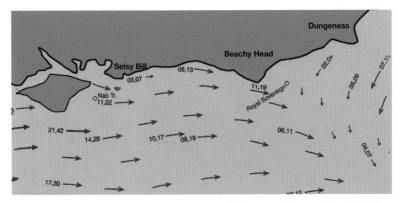

Catch the tides right and you can ride the incoming tidal stream all the way from the Eastern Solent to Dover.

You can also use the tides to advantage from the Solent to the Channel Islands. By riding the last of the ebb tide out past the Needles, you can time your arrival off Alderney 1–2 hours after high water, and have the strong Alderney Race carry you all the way to Guernsey. It is certainly worth doing you homework in advance.

Get the tides right and everyone will enjoy the voyage. Good planning is a key element.

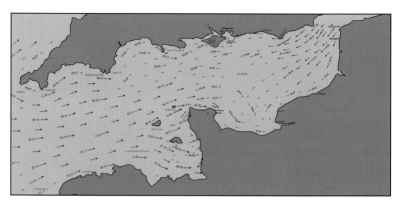

Tidal chart for the English Channel, 5 hours before HW Dover.

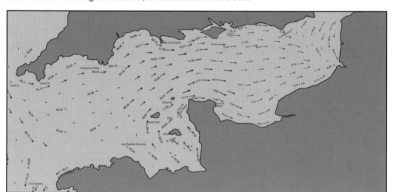

3 hours before HW Dover.

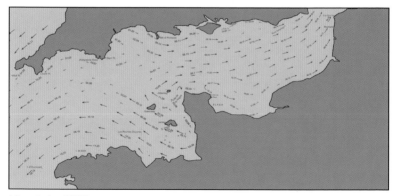

1 hour before HW Dover.

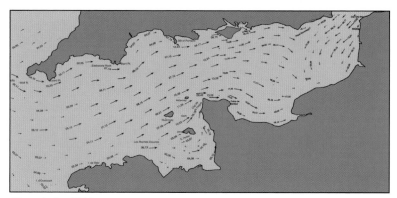

4 hours before HW Dover.

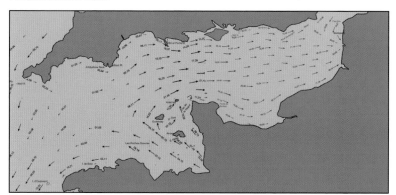

2 hours before HW Dover.

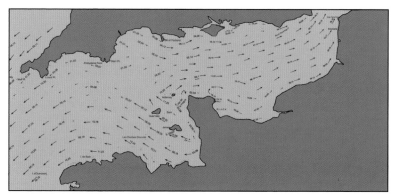

HW Dover.

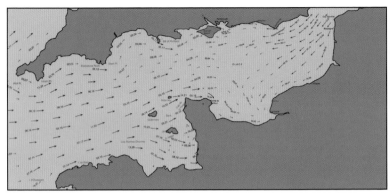

Tidal chart for the English Channel, 1 hour after HW Dover.

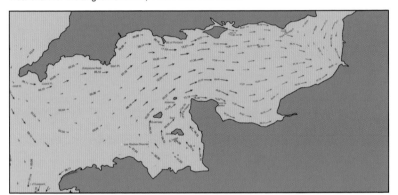

3 hours after HW Dover.

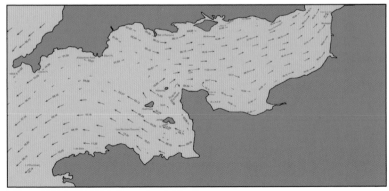

5 hours after HW Dover.

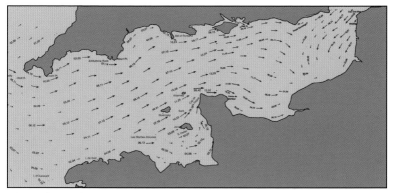

2 hours after HW Dover.

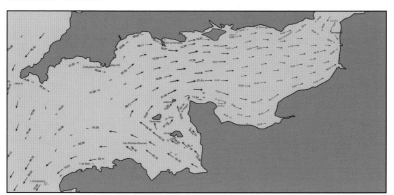

4 hours after HW Dover.

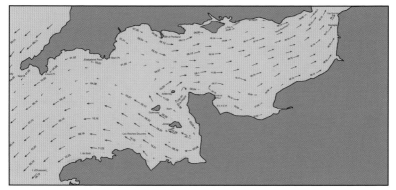

6 hours after HW Dover.

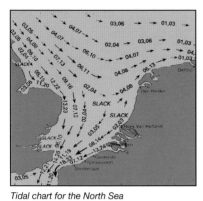

Tidal chart for the North Sea
5 hours before HW Dover.

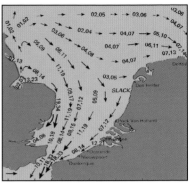

4 hours before HW Dover.

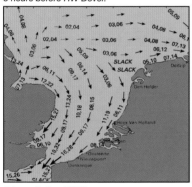

3 hours before HW Dover.

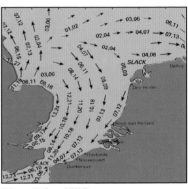

2 hours before HW Dover.

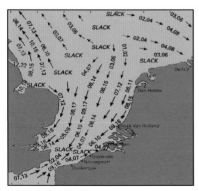

1 hour before HW Dover.

HW Dover.

1 hour after HW Dover.

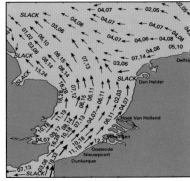

2 hours after HW Dover.

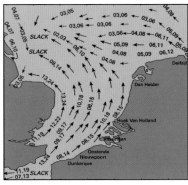

3 hours after HW Dover.

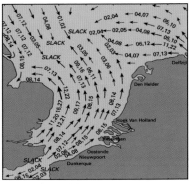

4 hours after HW Dover.

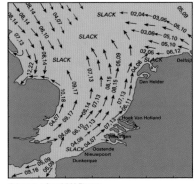

5 hours after HW Dover.

6 hours after HW Dover.

Distances between Channel ports	Longships	Falmouth	Fowey	Plymouth	Salcombe	Dartmouth	Torbay	Exmouth
Le Conquet	112	112	123	125	125	137	144	155
L'Aber Wrac'h	102	97	106	107	105	117	124	135
Roscoff	110	97	101	97	91	100	107	117
Trébeurden	120	105	106	102	94	102	109	120
Tréguier	132	112	110	101	94	98	102	112
Lézardrieux	142	121	118	107	94	100	105	114
St Quay-Portrieux	159	137	135	124	111	115	121	129
St Malo	172	149	146	133	118	120	124	132
St Helier	155	130	123	108	93	95	100	108
St Peter Port	139	113	104	89	73	70	75	81
Braye (Alderney)	146	116	106	89	72	69	71	75
Cherbourg	168	138	125	107	92	87	88	93
St Vaast	194	164	150	132	116	111	112	116
Ouistreham	229	189	185	167	151	146	147	147
Deauville	236	205	192	174	158	153	154	154
Le Havre	231	200	187	169	153	148	148	148
Fécamp	242	212	197	179	163	157	157	157
Dieppe	268	237	222	204	188	180	180	180
Boulogne	290	258	242	224	208	198	195	191
Calais	305	272	257	239	223	213	210	209

Needles	Nab Tower	Littlehampton	Shoreham	Brighton	Newhaven	Eastbourne	Rye	Folkstone	Dover
194	212	230	240	245	249	261	278	295	301
174	192	211	219	224	228	239	257	275	280
149	165	184	193	197	200	211	229	246	252
147	164	181	190	194	197	208	226	244	249
132	147	162	170	174	177	188	206	224	229
130	140	157	165	169	172	184	201	219	224
135	146	162	171	174	178	189	207	225	230
130	143	157	166	170	173	184	202	220	225
104	115	132	140	144	147	158	176	194	199
83	97	112	120	124	127	135	156	174	179
62	73	91	100	103	106	114	136	153	159
63	68	81	90	92	96	102	122	140	145
72	71	80	87	88	90	96	115	132	138
100	86	91	92	91	90	92	106	125	130
104	88	89	88	87	85	87	101	120	125
97	82	82	83	82	79	80	94	115	120
96	75	71	68	65	62	62	72	90	95
117	91	80	75	70	64	63	60	70	75
127	97	81	71	66	59	47	33	28	25
141	111	96	86	81	74	62	43	26	22

th Sea opens up all
ploring Amsterdam's
e small ports within
e sandy landscapes

Distances between North Sea ports	Lowestoft	Harwich	Brightlingsea	Burnham on Crouch	London Bridge	Sheerness	Ramsgate	Dover
Bremerhaven	284	309	327	336	382	340	323	336
Willhelmshaven	271	296	314	323	374	334	315	328
Deifzijl	218	243	261	270	320	280	262	275
Den Helder	118	147	165	174	222	180	161	174
Ijmuiden	104	126	144	151	199	157	144	155
Scheveningen	98	114	105	112	149	109	121	132
Roompotsluis	95	94	108	109	153	113	89	101
Vlissingen	99	100	106	115	149	109	85	92
Zeebruge	87	84	92	99	134	94	77	79
Ostend	87	77	88	92	125	85	65	65
Nieuport	89	80	86	93	126	86	58	58
Dunkirk	106	80	87	95	114	74	42	44

Going from Chichester to St Vaast-la-Hougue

Our late summer cruise to St Vaast-la-Hougue in our 27ft Rhodes 6 ton cruising yacht *Sea Jay* provides a good example on which to model preparations and execution of your own cross-Channel trip.

- Departure: Friday 25th September
- LW Portsmouth: 21:42 – 1.7m
- HW Portsmouth: 03:42 – 3.9m

St Vaast-la-Hougue is a modern harbour on the east of the Cherbourg peninsula that is easy to navigate to, with a 700 berth marina accessible 2 hours 15 mins before high water and 3 hours after. It is also a good start point for a cruise around the Seine Bay, with the delightful ports of Carentan Grandcamp, Isigny, Port-en-Bessin, Courseulles-sur-Mer, Ouistreham, Deauville, and best of all, Honfleur, a particular favourite that avoided the Allied pasting that flattened St Vaast during the Second World War.

St Vaast-la-Hougue with its 700 berth marina is an ideal start point for a cruise around the Seine Bay.

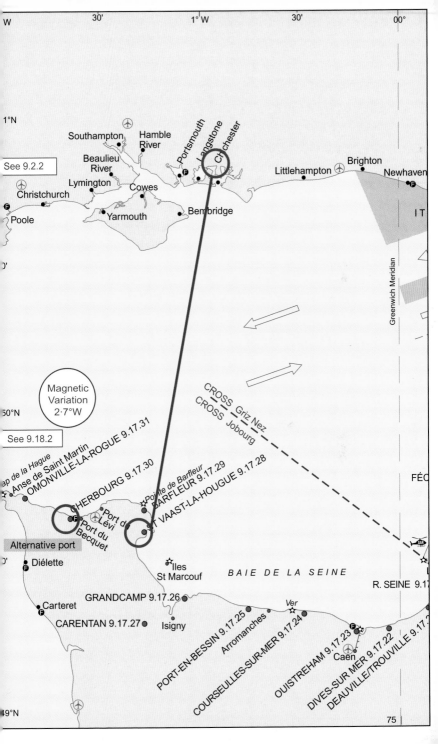

W

30' · 1°W · 30' · 00°

1°N

Southampton · Hamble River · Portsmouth · Langstone · Chichester · Littlehampton · Brighton · Newhaven

See 9.2.2

Beaulieu River
Lymington · Cowes
Christchurch
Poole · Yarmouth · Bembridge

I T

Greenwich Meridian

Magnetic Variation 2·7°W

50°N

See 9.18.2

CROSS Griz Nez
CROSS Jobourg

Cap de la Hague · Anse de Saint Martin · OMONVILLE-LA-ROGUE 9.17.31
CHERBOURG 9.17.30
Pointe de Barfleur · BARFLEUR 9.17.29
ST VAAST-LA-HOUGUE 9.17.28

FÉC

Port de Lévi
Port du Becquet

Alternative port

Diélette

Carteret

GRANDCAMP 9.17.26

CARENTAN 9.17.27 · Isigny

Iles St Marcouf · BAIE DE LA SEINE

R. SEINE 9.17

PORT-EN-BESSIN 9.17.25
Arromanches · Ver
COURSEULLES-SUR-MER 9.17.24
OUISTREHAM 9.17.23 · Caen
DIVES-SUR MER 9.17.22
DEAUVILLE/TROUVILLE 9.17

49°N

75

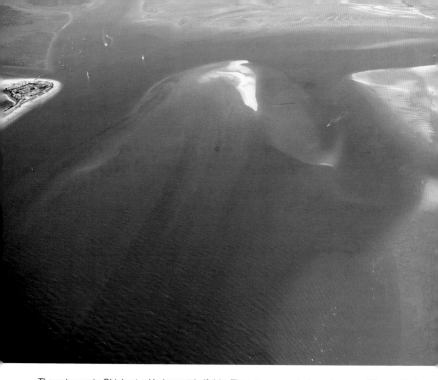

The entrance to Chichester Harbour at half tide. The entrance and channels are well buoyed but there is always at least one crew each weekend that finish up high and dry on the Winner Bank in the centre of the entrance.

Our plan had been to leave Chichester Marina at around 1900 to catch the the ebb and have a leisurely 1 hour sail down the harbour to give everyone a chance to settle in to the routines. We were to have had dinner anchored in the shelter of East Head where we were to brief everyone before setting off across the Channel at midnight.

But even the best-laid plans go awry, and delays forced us to have dinner on the pontoon outside the marina lock, and start our weekend cruise to St Vaast from the head of the harbour.

The forecast was for little wind, which pleased some of us but meant that we would be motor-sailing for much of the crossing. The good thing was that it was a beautiful clear night with the stars providing a welcome distraction from the noise of the engine. We timed our start to arrive off St Vaast close to high tide at 1335 on Saturday when the lock would be free flow into the marina.

Barfleur lighthouse, a sentinel that can be seen right across the Cherbourg peninsula.

Cherbourg was selected as the best alternative port in the event of fog or an emergency developing because it has easy access at all states of the tide and good shelter in the outer harbour should the weather defy the forecasts.

We passed the Chichester Bar beacon at 0030 and had the Nab Tower on our port beam an hour later, showing that we were averaging 5 knots over the ground with the tidal stream flooding up the Solent pushing us south east.

Rather than allow the chart plotter to dictate our course and continually correct for the tidal stream pushing us west later, we kept on a compass heading due south knowing that when the flood tide began to build after 0900, it would push us back onto the rhumb line. Adding to the navigation feel-good factor was the loom of St Catherine's lighthouse which stayed on our starboard quarter for the first half of the crossing, and we had the towering Barfleur lighthouse to steer towards during the second stage.

By 0600 just as dawn was breaking, we were crossing the west-going shipping separation channel, and by 0800, the second watch had the opportunity to ponder on where this constant stream of ships had come from and was going to on the easterly route up the Channel.

By 1030, our hourly plots on the chart showed that the ebb tide had swept us 7 miles west of the rhumb line, and that now the flow had changed direction, we were a little further up tide than we had wished. But up tide is the position you want to be, not down tide which would have left us punching into the stream running eastwards at 2 knots close inshore around the Cherbourg peninsular, which was soon pushing us back towards the rhumb line.

Had the weather turned inclement during the crossing, or the tidal stream pushed us further west than intended, we had the option heading to Cherbourg, our alternative port, 13 miles west of Barfleur Point.

There were no concerns on any account, and with Barfleur lighthouse standing out clearly on the horizon, we took advantage of a building northerly breeze to shake out the sails to make 5 knots on a broad reach around the Point.

By the time we had born off to run south down to Le Gravendest south cardinal buoy that marks the entrance to St Vaast, the breeze had built to a pleasant Force 3 and we arrived right on schedule at 1300. This is where we picked up our detailed pilotage plan listing course bearings and reference points that took us into the harbour to the marina. (See page 60.)

The return voyage on the Sunday afternoon was also timed to coincide with high water at St Vaast so that we could catch the first of the ebb running northwards to Barfleur lighthouse.

It also gave us time to sail in and take a look at Barfleur harbour before it dried out, but our crew became so excited by the large number of mackerel they were catching on a line of feathers trawled over the stern, that this late change of menu for dinner became a priority. Fresh fish grilled straight from the sea is an infinitely better proposition than the French steaks we had bought in the Saturday market at St Vaast!

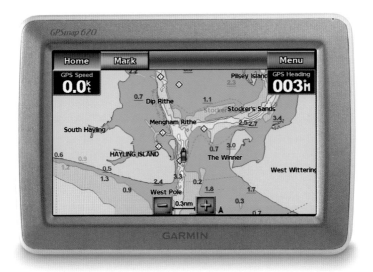

Chart plotters like this Garmin GPSMAP 620 multiscreen unit take all the guesswork out of picking up channel marks at night or in fog.

The fun of catching so many fish had the second benefit of taking minds off the prospect of seasickness and everyone was fine, even with the strong smell of cooking wafting up out of the companionway.

The north easterly winds were not the ideal direction for heading back to Chichester, but they died out at dusk and we were forced to drop sails and motor back across the Channel. On the plus side, we could at least steer a straight course which simplified the navigation.

This time we crossed the two shipping lanes at night. The Channel was as busy as ever, and without radar on *Sea Jay*, we found it difficult to judge the speed of this oncoming traffic. What looked to be clear one minute was patently not 5 mins later, and we learned to always steer for the stern of the nearest ship even if it meant changing course, because this just gave us time to cross the lane before the next ship came bearing down.

No sooner had we said good night to Barfleur's light, than the loom of St Catherine's lighthouse could just be seen when half way across the Channel. As we drew closer to the Isle of Wight, I was surprised by the

Back in home waters. Sea Jay and her crew crossing the bar into Chichester Harbour after a successful night crossing from St Vaast-la-Hougue.

large number of ships at anchor in the sheltered waters east of Sandown Bay, all waiting to berth in Southampton. Doubtless there are just as many there during the day, but lit like Christmas trees at night, they are so much more conspicuous.

The red lights marking the inner and outer bar beacons at the entrance to Chichester harbour are always hard to pick out amid the background clutter of lighting along Hayling Island's seafront, but our trusty Garmin chart plotter took all the guesswork out of the approach.

Our insistence on making the most of the fading ENE breeze rather than turning on the engine the previous evening, added several hours to the voyage. But that was no bad thing, because we arrived back in Chichester harbour in daylight, admittedly punching an outgoing tide, and lazed the rest of the day anchored up in the seclusion of Thorney Channel, cooking the French steaks we had bought in St Vaast, and quietly sampling the stock of French wines we had brought back with us. A great ending to what for most of the crew had been an adventurous first foreign cruise.

Get the kids involved, but think safety. Note the lifejacket and lifeline attached to the fore and aft jackstay.

Going from the Solent to the Dutch Waddenzee

The following extract is from the log of Minke II, *a Halberg Rassy 36 owned by Tim Bishop.*

Family commitments limited our summer cruise to discover the Dutch Frisian Islands and inland sea to a strict two-week timetable. We just didn't have enough time to sit around and wait for the right 'weather window' for the long bash across the North Sea, and set out from Yarmouth on the Isle of Wight running before a rain-laden Force 4 to overnight in Brighton marina.

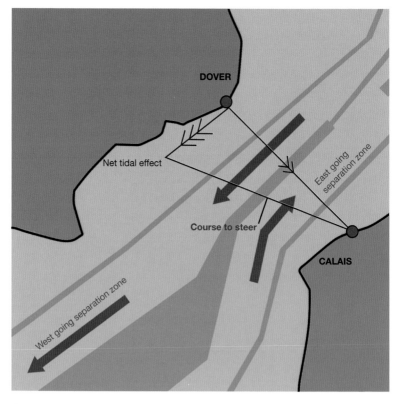

Crossing the Channel at its narrowest point between Dover and Calais can usually be done in one tide. Draw in the net tide vector west or east to give you the course to steer.

We timed our start to coincide with the east-going tidal stream that would carry us all the way to Dover and at least ensure relatively smooth seas even if it blew up harder later. If the weather became too inclement, Littlehampton, accessible 2 hours either side of low water, would be our alternative port en-route to Brighton.

The following morning, the south westerly winds were still fairly strong, but by timing our departure to run with the tidal stream, conditions were not expected to be any worse than the previous day. This time, Eastbourne, Rye, Folkstone and Dover were our intended refuge ports should conditions deteriorate.

Crossing the English Channel between Dover and Calais is like walking across a motorway. This is the busiest shipping zone in the world, but it is also the shortest route across the Channel – and densely policed. Everyone is alert and ships' bridges are fully manned.

It is by far the safest place for a small vessel to cross. Rather than stop in Dover we set out in the early hours, just as the tide had started to ebb, to cross the traffic separation zones in daylight and make sure we would be off Calais before nightfall.

Calais is a very complex port and, like Zeebrugge, needs good concentration. Niewport is a good refuge port, particularly when there is a strong south westery blowing. Indeed, this whole coastal strip is well protected from south westerlies, and having timed it so that we had the tide under us, we preferred to make the 2-day passage to Ijmuiden in one hit.

The stretch between Calais and Ostend is littered with shoals but they are easy to follow with a chart plotter and echo sounder. Off Niewport the winds and sea flattened out as we ran ENE with 2–3 knots of fair tide, giving us 8–9 knots over the ground.

While the BBC shipping forecast was predicting strong winds, the German forecast for the German Bight, broadcast in English, proved much more accurate. The DWD forecast downloaded on a NASA Weatherman is equally accurate but available only in German. However, wind direction/strength arrows are universal, making it easy to read.

The low-pressure systems generally move up the English Channel at around 25 knots, giving you plenty of warning to head for alternative ports like Ostend, Zeebrugge or Breskens should the need arise.

Europort is second only to Shanghai in the league of shipping ports, so the waters surrounding the entrance to the Waterweg are amongst the busiest in the world. To cross the entrance you must first get permission from Maas Central, then go flat out, because they give you very little time to make the crossing. We found it best to wait and follow a local boat. Beware the bow waves from passing ships too. *Minke II* crashed into one or two of these standing waves, which sent 7–8 tons of green water down the decks.

The entrance to Ijmuiden is not a good refuge for small boats when the winds are west of north. It is wide open from the north and a wall, lined with concrete pill boxes designed to keep the Brits at bay, takes the full force of the seas – and any vessels that get swept up against it!

There is always a large number of ships lit like Christmas trees in an anchor zone outside the entrance, waiting their turn to pass through the Noordzeekanaal to Amsterdam, together with a large wind farm to contend

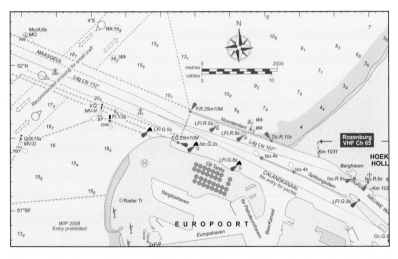

Entrance to the Europort, the second busiest port in the world. You must get permission to cross the shipping channel, then go flat out because you are given very little time to do so.

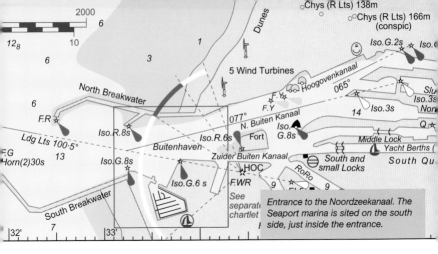

with. The radar trace thrown up by the windmills is very bright, but the solitary red light on the top of each one is not. Moreover, the cardinal buoyage system surrounding them looks more like trawlers than buoys. Not something to be passing by at night!

The wind farm close to the entrance to the Noordzeekanaal. The blades offer a strong radar trace but their lights and the cardinal buoyage around them is not as good.

This is marina berthing Dutch style. You can often walk from one side of the harbour to the other simply by walking across the boats!

The weather held just long enough to run up the entrance and tie up in the Seaport marina on the south side. Dutch marinas are very cheap, but you get very little for your money. Everyone rafts up against each other and the sheer mass of boats often allows you to walk from one side of the harbour to the other.

The Dutch are very skilled at handling their boats in tight situations, but give no quarter, and readily rush to be first into any opening. Timidity gets you nowhere. You quickly learn to push or be pushed, with a firm hand on the gear lever and fenders at the ready.

Just be prepared for when the hydrofoil ferries pass close by at 30 knots or for the huge intimidating ships that may share a canal with you. There is no charge for passing through the locks, but the keepers do have a clog they let down on a fishing line to collect tips.

Beware of these fast moving hydrofoil ferries running up and down the Noordzeekanaal...

... and the much bigger cruise ships and cargo vessels that share the same narrow waterway!

Minke II's *course up through the Ijsselmeer and sandy inlets of the Waddenzee to the Frisian Islands and back to Amsterdam.*

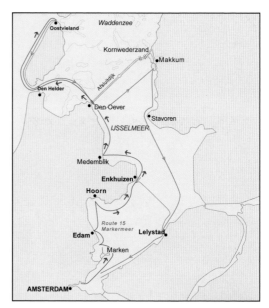

Navigating through the Dutch locks requires nerves of steel; the locals give no quarter in the race through the gates.

Once through the locks and into the Ijsselmeer, the water traffic becomes much less frenetic.

A tidal atlas of the Waddenzee is both essential and a legal requirement to have onboard. The pilot book is especially useful in helping to identify one withy-marked passage from another in what is otherwise an empty sea. We found these inshore passages all beautifully marked, especially the route to Oost Vlieland, the jewel of the Frisian islands, when our echo sounder consistently read 0.5m under *Minke II's* keel.

Exiting at Ijmuiden, we braced ourselves for the hard slog against the prevailing winds back to the Solent. This is not for the faint hearted or seasickness sufferers, even with the promise of an overnight stopover in Niewport, enroute.

Thankfully, there are hourly flights back to England both from Schippol and Rotterdam to ease the burden. Our kids simply hunkered down under duvets in the double berth astern to watch DVDs and play computer games. It never ceases to amaze me how time flies by when you are otherwise engaged!

Sunset across a sandy inlet within the Frisian Islands close to Oost Vlieland, the jewel within this Dutch archipelago.

Keep to the channels in the Waddenzee. The woman seemingly walking on water in this picture illustrates just how deceptive the sand banks are.

Kids can keep themselves amused for hours with computer games and DVDs, especially on overnight crossings.

Going from Hamble to St Peter Port

The following extract is from the log of Madhatta, *a* Fairlaine Phantom *owned by John and Sahra Gott.*

This is a favourite cruise for powerboat (and sailboat) owners who use it as an excuse to fill their tanks with duty free fuel, as well as enjoy a great destination. We made a trip over the weekend starting Saturday 25th July, when the rising tide allowed a later afternoon arrival into St Peter Port. The trip coincided with Spring tides, so it was important to reach the Alderney Race (where the stream can run at up to 9 knots) just before high water when the tide is slack, to minimise the wind-against-tide effect through the Race.

Dover 25th July		St Peter Port		Dover 26th July	
HW	0059 UT 6.8m	LW	1509 UT 0.8m	HW	0143 UT 6.7m
LW	0839 UT 0.7m	HW	2105 UT 9.8m	LW	0917 UT 0.7m
HW	1316 UT 7.0m			HW	1400 UT 6.9m
LW	2100 UT 0.5m			LW	2139 UT 0.5m

Forecast: West or South West Force 3, increasing to Force 4 later. Slight or Moderate. Showers. Good.

Not the best of forecasts, but with a high pressure system over Biscay promising to push the approaching low up over Ireland and Scotland, we decided that we could complete the voyage before the cold front came through.

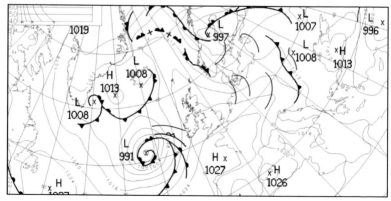

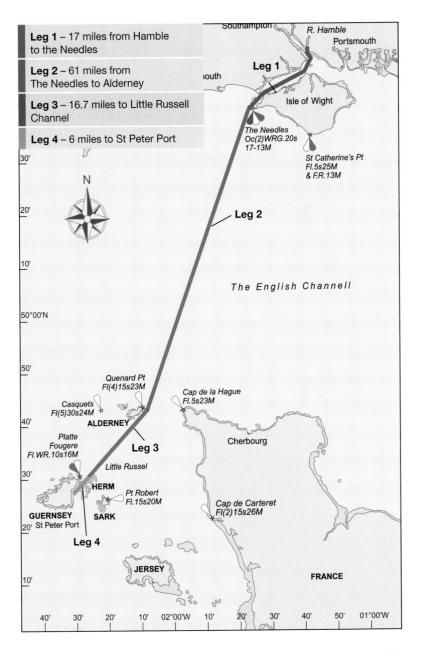

Leg 1 – 17 miles from Hamble to the Needles

Leg 2 – 61 miles from The Needles to Alderney

Leg 3 – 16.7 miles to Little Russell Channel

Leg 4 – 6 miles to St Peter Port

Southampton

R. Hamble

Portsmouth

Leg 1

iouth

Isle of Wight

The Needles
Oc(2)WRG.20s
17-13M

St Catherine's Pt
Fl.5s25M
& F.R.13M

Leg 2

The English Channel

N

Quenard Pt
Fl(4)15s23M

Cap de la Hague
Fl.5s23M

Casquets
Fl(5)30s24M

ALDERNEY

Platte
Fougere
Fl.WR.10s16M

Leg 3

Cherbourg

Little Russel

HERM

Pt Robert
Fl.15s20M

GUERNSEY

SARK

St Peter Port

Cap de Carteret
Fl(2)15s26M

Leg 4

JERSEY

FRANCE

50°00'N

01°00'W

02°00'W

Aerial view of St Peter Port, a favourite weekend destination for powerboat crews.

The ideal time to arrive off Alderney was 1300 UT. Working back, the 61 mile leg 2 from the Needles was expected to take 4 hours 6 minutes at an average speed of 15 knots. That dictated that we needed to exit the Needles Channel close to 0900 UT, giving us the option of either leaving Hamble just after 0730 UT or breaking the voyage by motoring across to spend Friday night in Yarmouth, Isle of Wight, ready for a more social start on Saturday morning. We chose the latter to give us time to go through our checks and briefing, and get everyone accustomed to being onboard in the safer confines of the Solent.

Our trip coincided with the summer equinox, and with the possibility of a bumpy crossing when the winds were opposing the very strong tidal stream, we included Poole together with Braye Harbour, Alderney as refuge ports within our plan. We reached the Alderney Race on schedule at 1300 UT and covered the 16.7 miles down to the entrance to the Russel Channel an hour later.

Madhatta has a draft of 1m, and looking up the depth table for St Peter Port in *Reeds Nautical Almanac*, it was clear that we would not be able to get over the marina sill until after 1800 UT.

This left us with the option of slowing down during leg 4 through the Little Russel Channel, or continuing at 15 knots and tying up on the outer visitor pontoon, putting the kettle on and waiting for the tide to rise. With the

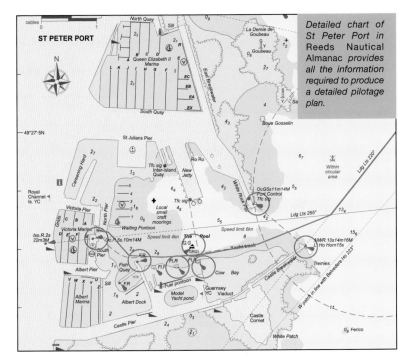

Detailed chart of St Peter Port in Reeds Nautical Almanac *provides all the information required to produce a detailed pilotage plan.*

cold front coming through, the decision was taken not to hang about. We changed from passage plan to pilotage plan for the final 6 mile leg. *Reeds Nautical Almanac* warns: 'Off-lying dangers, a big tidal range (up to 9.4m) and strong tidal streams demand careful navigation. Beware also the ferries and shipping. This is a busy commercial port and shipping has right of way at all times.'

The harbour speed limit is 6 knots between the outer pier heads to a line south from New Jetty to Castle Pier. West of this line, the limit is 4 knots. We were greeted by the marina launch which directed us straight to the waiting pontoon, then escorted us into the marina once the tide had risen sufficiently above the sill.

The trip was a success. Thanks to thorough planning, we had dodged in ahead of an approaching weather system to reach our destination on time without surprises, or the need to use our ports of refuge.

Arrival
and return

Flag etiquette

Ensigns

The ensign flown from a staff at the stern or a third of the way up the backstay, denotes a vessel's nationality. The traditional British maritime flag is the Red ensign, and legally, must be flown when entering or leaving a foreign port. The White ensign, Blue ensign and Defaced Red and Blue ensigns can only be flown on yachts owned by members of privilged yacht clubs, and who carry a warrant onboard allowing them to do so.

The correct times to fly the ensign are between 0800 local time (0900 between 1st November and 14th February) and sunset or 2100, whichever is earlier. It should also be furled when leaving the vessel un-manned.

The Red ensign is the standard national maritime flag marking the nationality of a British vessel.

The White ensign is exclusive to Royal Navy vessels and yachts belonging to members of the Royal Yacht Squadron.

The Blue ensign can only be flown by members of certain yacht clubs and is subject to a warrant issued by the club on behalf of the Secretary of State for Defence. The warrant is personal to the owner and the ensign can only be flown when he or she is on board, or in effective control of the vessel – and only in conjunction with the relevant club burgee.

The Blue and Red ensign defaced with a club burgee is subject to exactly the same rules as the Blue ensign above.

The ensign should not be flown overnight unless the vessel is approaching or leaving port. The correct times to fly a maritime flag are between 0800 local time (0900 between 1st November and 14th February) and sunset or 2100, whichever is earlier. It should be furled whenever all the crew leave the vessel.

Dipping the ensign

It is traditional for vessels to salute Royal yachts and warships of any nationality. The salute is made by dipping the ensign two-thirds of the way down the staff. This can also be achieved by taking the staff out of its holder and manually dipping the staff with the flag attached. The vessel saluted should respond by dipping her ensign and rehoisting it. The saluting vessel can then re-hoist her ensign. It is also customary for a Flag Officer to be saluted by a yacht flying the burgee of that club – but only once a day!

Courtesy flag

It is traditional, though not obligatory, to fly the maritime flag of a country as a mark of courtesy when visiting its waters. The correct position on a single-masted yacht is from the starboard crosstrees. All other burgees, house flags and pennants should be flown from the port crosstrees. If a motor cruiser does not have a dedicated signal halyard, a prominent position such as the VHF aerial is a good enough substitute to fly flags from.

The Dutch courtesy flag flown from the starboard spreader.

Q flag

The yellow Q flag requesting Customs clearance, should also be flown from the starboard spreader above the courtesy ensign until the vessel has been cleared by Customs and Immigration. The Q flag is then replaced by the courtesy flag.

The Q flag is not required when sailing from one EU port to another unless you have duty free goods to declare or non-EU nationals onboard. A UK registered vessel need fly it only when entering or returning from a non-EU country – which includes the Channel Islands. You must obtain Customs and Immigration clearance for both the boat and crew before anyone leaves the boat on any other business. To contact your local Customs office call the National Advice Line: +44 (0)845 010 9000.

Dressed overall

Vessels are dressed overall at celebratory events like Royal birthdays, regattas and festivals but beware the order in which they are hoisted. Some years ago, the local Police Commissioner was left red-faced when Sir Alec Rose, the guest of honour at a Police function, asked him quietly, 'The flag signals read 'BIG TIT'. Do you think that refers to you or me?'

The bunting, dressed from bow to masthead and down the stern, should be made up of international signals only. The correct order is:

E-Q-p3-G-p8-Z-p4-W-p6-P-p1-I-ANSWER-T-Y-B-X-1st SUB-H-3rd SUB-D-F-2nd SUB-U-A-O-M-R-p2-J-p0-N-p9-K-p7-V-p5-L-C-S

Customs formalities

Departing the UK

If you are departing the UK and going directly to another EU country, you are free of formalities with UK Customs. Only if you are going directly to a non-EU country or the Channel Islands should you advise Customs of your intentions by completing form C1331. This can be downloaded directly from www.hmce.gov.uk/forms or by calling the National Advice Line: +44 (0) 845 010 9000. The form should also be readily available from marina offices and yacht clubs.

Dressed overall, but are the flags in the right order?

Part (I) of the form must be completed and returned to Customs before leaving the UK, either by handing it to a Customs officer, placing it in a Customs post box in the marina or port or phoning the Customs National Yachtline +44 (0) 845 723 1110. If, having completed form C1331, your departure is delayed, you must advise Customs by writing to the Customs location where the original C1331 was sent. If the voyage is abandoned, you must endorse Part (ii) of the Form C1331 with the words 'voyage abandoned'.

Duty free stores: You are only eligible to carry duty-free goods bought from a bonded store if you are going to a port south of Brest or north of the river Eider in Denmark. If you meet these criteria, then you must complete Form C945 and take or fax it to the local Customs office before loading duty free stores. They will normally be placed under Customs seal on board and must not be opened in UK waters without paying Customs charges. You will also be liable to pay if you interrupt or abandon your voyage.

Immigration requirements: You do not need to notify Immigration if your first port of call is expected to be in the Irish Republic, Channel Islands or elsewhere in the EU. Only when the first port of call is outside the EU, or you are carrying someone who has no right of abode in the EU, do you need to notify an Immigration officer in advance. In some locations, the Customs officer also acts as an Immigration official. Contact your local Customs office or call the National Advice Line: Tel: +44 (0) 845 010 9000.

Taking pets abroad: Although UK quarantine rules have been relaxed, pets can only be brought back to the UK by an authorised carrier or route unless you are voyaging directly from the Channel Islands or Ireland. This does not include private boats or planes, so you will need to make separate arrangements when returning to the UK. Details of the correct method of carrier and routes can be gained from the Pets Helpline. Tel: +44 (0) 870 241 1710.

The Schengen Convention: Some EU and Nordic countries, though not the UK, have dispensed with border controls. These include Belgium, Denmark, Finland, Germany, Iceland, Italy, the Netherlands, Norway, Portugal, Spain and Sweden. As a result, you may be asked for a crew list and passport information, but since the UK's laws and practices do not differentiate in any way between Schengen member and non-member countries, in practice, port authorities are just as likely to wave you on.

Returning to the UK

The booze cruise – what can I bring back?
Returning from any EU port
Legally, you can bring back as much EU duty paid goods as you like, so long as they are for your own use or gifts for family and friends. You cannot bring back goods for commercial purposes or for payment in kind. Goods, for instance, cannot be brought back for family and friends if they contribute anything towards their cost or your travel expenses.

Pets can only be brought back into the UK by an authorised carrier which does not include private boats. If you have to take your pets with you on a voyage abroad, then you will need to make separate arrangements to bring them back into the UK.

If you bring back large quantities of alcohol or tobacco, questions may be asked about your trip, your purchases and the purpose for which you hold the goods. If they are for a wedding or celebration, then inviting the Customs men to the party may save you problems later.

Guideline limits for personal consumption
■ 3,200 cigarettes
■ 400 cigarillos
■ 200 cigars
■ 3kg of smoking tobacco
■ 110 litres of beer
■ 10 litres of spirits
■ 90 litres of wine
■ 20 litres of fortified wine

Returning from outside the EU
The Customs allowance for travellers over the age of 17 is:

■ **Alcohol:** 1 litre of spirits or strong liqueurs (over 22% volume), or 2 litres of fortified wine (such as port or sherry), sparkling wine or any other alcoholic beverage of less than 22% volume.

■ You can combine these allowances, provided you do not exceed your total alcohol allowance. For example, if you only bring back 1 litre of fortified wine (50% of your full allowance of 2 litres), you may also bring back half a litre of spirits (50% of the full allowance).

■ In addition, you may also bring back 16 litres of beer and 4 litres of still wine.

■ Tobacco: 200 cigarettes, or 100 cigarillos, or 50 cigars, or 250g of tobacco.

Other goods: Passengers travelling by private boat for pleasure purposes are only entitled to an allowance of £240.

Banned items: Drugs, meat, dairy products, most fruits, vegetables, seeds and bulbs.

When to fly the Q flag: Returning from another EU country, there is no need to fly a Q flag or notify customs of your arrival if all the crew reside within the EU. Anyone on board who is not an EU national must get an Immigration officer's permission to enter the UK. The skipper is responsible for making sure that they do. You will need to contact the nearest Immigration office by telephone to arrange clearance. The Customs officer to whom you report your arrival to will be able to advise on this.

You must fly the Q flag from the 12 nautical mile territorial waters limit when returning from outside the EU or Channel Islands. Report to Customs by telephoning the National Yachtline on +44 (0) 845 723 1110 and completing form C1331. No one can leave the vessel until it has been cleared by a Customs official.

Back home! If you have returned from the Channel Islands or outside the EU, or have non-EU crewmembers onboard, you must fly a Q flag, report to Customs and not leave the vessel until you have been cleared by a Customs official.

8 The crew

Safety first. That has to be the watchword onboard whether sailing or motoring. A safety briefing should precede any voyage and it needs to be fun. A few amusing anecdotes sprinkled in to a pre-flight check by cabin staff always gets attention. The same applies when addressing your crew. A good briefing will give them confidence that you know what you are doing. If you can involve the Mate in any demonstrations, he or she will share their confidence too.

The safety briefing should include operating the radio, firing flares and man overboard routines, as well as when to wear lifejackets. There is a limit as to how long people can concentrate, so split the briefing into two parts: below decks, and on deck.

The first rule onboard: One hand for the ship – And one for yourself!

Safety briefing

Chart table:	Show where charts, almanac, pilot books and binoculars are stowed.
Fire extinguishers/ fire blanket:	Where are they?
First-aid kit:	Where is it?
Heads:	How to use the loo and its seacocks.
Oven/hob:	Gas taps and gimbles. Show how they work. Turn off after use.
Seacocks:	Galley, engine intake etc.
VHF radio:	Call sign routine. Demonstrate by calling Coastguard for a radio check and display a procedure card by the radio.
Water:	Supplies are limited. Use water sparingly.

On deck

Bilge pumps:	Where they are and how do you operate them?
Dinghy:	How do you get in and out of it safely
Engine:	How do you stop and start it?
Flares:	Where are they stored, how do you fire them and when?
Horseshoe buoy:	How do you throw it?
Danbuoy:	How do you launch it?
Lifejacket and harness:	When are they worn? Where are they stored How to put them on
Jackstays:	How and where to hook on
Liferaft:	Where is it and how do you release it?
Man overboard drill:	Plan a practice with all the crew
Final question:	Can everyone swim?

Clothing

Cruising offshore requires rather more protection than when taking a spin around a harbour. During an overnight passage, clothing has to keep you warm and dry in the cold of night as well as during the day. When comfort is a priority, don't skimp on cost as clothing manufacturers have gone to great lengths to develop clothing systems to cope with these climatic extremes. Children get cold much quicker than adults, so make sure they keep warm and dry – and have plenty to keep them occupied.

Staying warm and keeping dry are really two sides of the same coin as far as thermal insulation is concerned. Cotton underclothes, for instance, can absorb up to 100% of their own weight in water or sweat, and with this moisture next to the skin, body heat is sapped out 30 times faster than with a dry fabric. By contrast, hollow fibred polyester thermal undergarments have the unique ability to wick perspiration away from the skin into the outer garments and keep the skin warm and dry.

Many sail wear manufacturers now produce fully-breathable outer garments designed to keep you dry both from spray and the inner moisture generated by body heat during exertions like grinding a winch or hoisting a sail. But if the voyage is simply a casual taster for the sport, no one will expect you to go out and spend out on specialist clothing.

Ask the skipper if you can borrow oilskins, and if not, good ski-wear will suffice. The boat should be equipped with sufficient lifejackets for all the crew so you should not need to worry on this count either. Simply pack clothes that will keep you warm.

The wind, salt water spray and sun reflected on the water combine to accentuate sunburn and will dry out the skin much more than when you on dry land. Remember to slap on plenty of high factor sun screen, wear sunglasses and slip on a t-shirt.

The decks can get very wet and slippery, so good boots or sailing shoes with non-slip soles are another priority. Footwear with closed toes will save you from tripping on the many hazards on deck when it is all too easy to stub a toe.

Dressed for the part: Full oilskins, lifejacket with crotch straps, safety lines, hat and gloves. You can always peel off layers later when the weather is right.

Watch systems

If you are sailing overnight or longer, then the crew need to be divided up into watches. It is often simplest to divide the crew into two teams and have the skipper, navigator, and, if you are lucky, the cook, all floating between the watches ready to be called on to help. Watch times are very much a personal preference to be discussed with the crew. Some like to divide the day into four 6-hour periods. Others prefer to reduce the night shifts into 4-hour stints, which has the advantage of moving the watch groups up one time schedule each day, rotating the worst 'night-watchman' hours.

Typical watch system
0800–1400 – Port watch
1400–2000 – Starboard watch
2000–0000 – Port watch
0000–0400 – Starboard watch
0400–0800 – Port watch
0800–1400 – Starboard watch

Night watches need to be woken with hot drinks 15–20 minutes before they are due on deck, and daylight watches 40 minutes before to give them time to have a meal. The ongoing watch should put on their oilskins, lifejackets and harnesses before going on deck and clip on before leaving the companionway unless briefed otherwise. Another safety precaution is to have each crew member call out their name as they come on deck during the night, and again before they go below.

Safety briefing: Let the crew handle items like flares and explain how they operate.

Using a VHF radio

It is a good idea to show your crew how to operate the radio before you leave harbour. It also makes sense to post encapsulated instruction cards close by, listing the vessel's call sign and a phonetic alphabet, together with normal and emergency call routines as shown on the following pages.

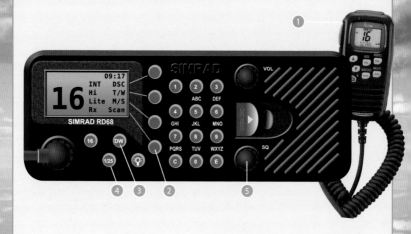

① Press to talk (PTT) microphone. Press the PTT button and the set will switch from receive to transmit. Hold the microphone 5cm from your mouth and speak clearly. Say 'Over' at the end of the message and remember to release the PTT button.

② Scan. To select and monitor several channels at one time.

③ DW (Dual Watch). To monitor priority channel 16 and one other channel.

④ High/low power. Use low power for routine calls.

⑤ Squelch. Filter reduces background noise. Adjust knob until interference is barely audible.

DSC Routine Call

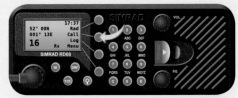

1 Select **call**.

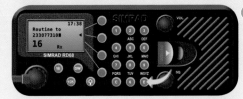

2 Enter **MMSI**.

3 Select **Intership Channel**
6, 8, 72 or 77.

4 Press **Send**, then **E** to confirm.

5 Wait for acknowledgment then transmit using low power.
'*Madhatta*. This is *Sea Jay.*'
Our ETA at Cowes is now 1500. Over.'

Call sign routine

THIS IS THE YACHT *SEA JAY*'
(call sign) 'TWO... BRAVO...MIKE...WHISKEY... EIGHT'
'CALLING' (Coastguard/other vessel by name etc.)
'DO YOU READ?'

Wait for 1 minute before repeating

Once a call is acknowledged, the recipient will nominate another channel to continue communication. If you fail to connect on this channel, return to Channel 16 and repeat the routine.

Phonetic alphabet

Use the phonetic alphabet to spell out abbreviations, call signs, words and vessel names.

A	ALPHA	N	NOVEMBER
B	BRAVO	O	OSCAR
C	CHARLIE	P	PAPA
D	DELTA	Q	QUEBEC
E	ECHO	R	ROMEO
F	FOXTROT	S	SIERRA
G	GOLF	T	TANGO
H	HOTEL	U	UNIFORM
I	INDIA	V	VICTOR
J	JULIET	W	WHISKEY
K	KILO	X	X-RAY
L	LIMA	Y	YANKEE
M	MIKE	Z	ZULU

Mayday routine – how to call on Channel 16 in a distress situation

1. Open the red cover.

2. Press red button.

3. Select cause of distress, if there is time.

4. Press and hold the red button through the countdown.

5. Wait 15 seconds for the acknowledgement. Send voice Mayday on Channel 16 using high power.

Emergency radio routine

There are three levels of emergency call:

First Level Emergency: 'MAYDAY – MAYDAY – MAYDAY!'
The distress signal is to be used only when there is grave danger to boat or crew.

Second Level Emergency: 'PAN-PAN – PAN-PAN – PAN-PAN!'
This urgency signal should be used when there is a serious, but not life threatening situation that requires assistance, including:
- Serious illness or injury.
- The skipper is incapacitated.
- You are in danger of being swept ashore by high seas or currents.

Third Level Emergency: 'SECURITY – SECURITY – SECURITY!'
This signal is used to warn of conditions that may affect other sailors in the area, including:
- Notify hazards to navigation ie drifting containers, logs or nets.
- Warning from large vessel entering a narrow channel.
- You have broken down or run out of fuel.
- You have a rope round your prop.

High and dry on a falling tide. This skipper dozed off at the wheel. Unless someone has been injured, this is not a life threatening situation and should be treated as a third level emergency.

Making an emergency call

Start with level of emergency	'MAYDAY – MAYDAY – MAYDAY!'
Your vessel's type and name, repeated 3 times.	'THIS IS THE YACHT *SEA JAY*'...x3
The position of your boat, latitude and longitude...	'WE ARE IN POSITION (lat and long)'...x2
....or bearing and distance from a headland or landmark.	'BEARING xxx xxx MILES FROM xxx
The nature of your problem.	'WE ARE SINKING / HAVE A MAN OVERBOARD / INJURED CREWMAN etc'
The number of persons on board and if there are any injuries (specify)	WE HAVE xx PEOPLE ONBOARD, xx WITH INJURIES
Description of vessel, including:	
Size:	WE ARE: 27 FEET (8,23 METRES)
Colour:	VARNISHED MAHOGANY
Type of vessel:	MOTORYACHT/SAILING YACHT

Man Overboard (MOB)

Things happen fast when someone falls overboard. Within a minute, a yacht moving at just 6 knots will have travelled 600ft (182m). If a motor vessel is travelling at 20 knots, then the distance will have widened to 2,000ft (610m), which is further than you can see a small object from deck level in a heavy swell. The need is for fast, clear, co-ordinated action. Regular crew practice not only highlights the routines for recovery but focuses minds on prevention.

The first rule is to wear a lifejacket and clip your lifeline on whenever you have to go out on deck in heavy weather or at night. These are the fundamentals whether you are motoring or sailing:

Have you practised man overboard drill? What if it is the skipper that falls over the side? Do other members of the crew have the knowledge and ability to turn the boat round and pick you up?

STOP THE VESSEL

RAISE THE ALARM BY SHOUTING 'MAN OVERBOARD!'

Locate the MOB casualty

- One person keeps the casualty in sight, continually pointing in their direction
- Throw the danbuoy, horseshoe lifebelt or a large fender overboard
- Press the 'MOB' and then 'ENTER' buttons on the GPS
- Start the recovery manoeuvre (see following sections)
- In darkness, use a searchlight to illuminate search area
- Send a MAYDAY call on the VHF, satellite phone or DSC alert

What to do if YOU are the MOB

- Keep calm
- Inflate your lifejacket and turn its light on
- Kick off your boots
- Locate the boat and wave to show you are OK
- Pull up your hood on your jacket or lifejacket if spray is making it difficult to breath
- Locate the floatation device thrown from the vessel and hold on to it
- Use your whistle to make sound signals
- Save your energy – Do not try to swim or shout
- Take up the HELP (foetal) position to retain core body heat

Recovery of MOB

- Ready a rope to lasso around the MOB
- Pull the MOB to lowest part of boat – the bathing platform or cockpit
- Attach the boarding ladder or step fender
- Grab the MOB by the collar or lifejacket and pull them onboard

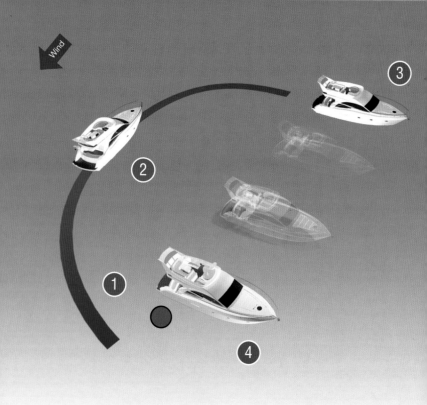

Close quarters recovery

Casualty (⬤) falls overboard.

1 Shout 'MAN OVERBOARD' to alert the crew. Press MOB button on GPS. Stop to gauge wind direction. One crew keeps pointing at the MOB to provide visual reference for helm.

2 Turn bows and drive upwind.

3 Turn and stop when you have the boat wind abeam of the MOB.

4 Drift downwind onto the MOB. Use the engine furthest away from MOB to adjust your position.

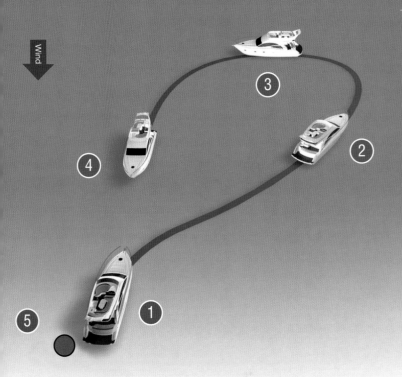

Williamson turn

Casualty (●) falls overboard.

1. Shout 'MAN OVERBOARD!' to alert the crew. Press MOB button on GPS. One crew keeps pointing at the MOB to provide visual reference for helm. Note compass course and calculate a reciprocal course.

2. Steer 60° away to port or starboard to open up room to turn full circle and return down your own wake.

3. Turn the helm hard over until boat is near to the reciprocal course then straighten up.

4. Follow your wake back, slow down and search for the MOB.

5. When located, turn beam on to the wind and drift down onto the MOB as per the close quarters recovery method, opposite. Use the engine furthest away from the MOB to adjust your position.

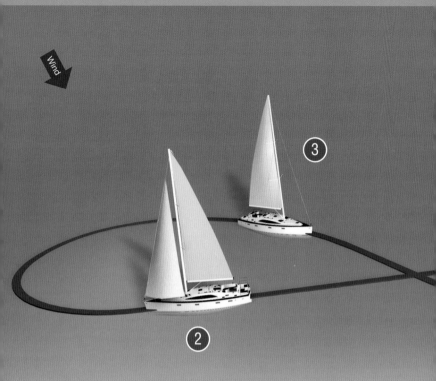

Man overboard recovery using engine

Casualty (⬤) falls overboard.

1 Shout 'MAN OVERBOARD!' to alert the crew. Press MOB button on GPS. One crew keeps pointing at the MOB to provide visual reference for helm.

2 'Heave to' by coming up to wind and prepare to tack, leaving the headsail backed and mainsail hauled in. Check that no lines are over the side and start the engine.

3 Drop the headsail and motor to leeward of the MOB.

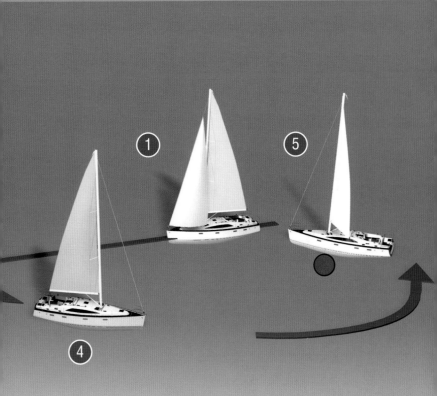

④ Prepare to approach the MOB to windward so that boat is blown down on to the MOB. The rescuing party must be forward of the shrouds so as not to be injured by the boom.

⑤ De-power the mainsail by releasing the kicking strap and letting the sheet out until the sail flaps. Recover the MOB on leeward side of the yacht.

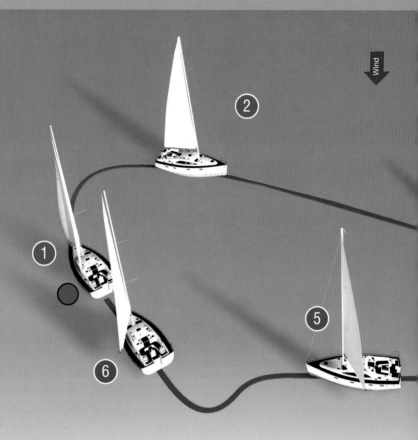

Man overboard recovery under sail

Casualty (●) falls overboard.

1 Shout 'MAN OVERBOARD!' to alert the crew. Press MOB button on GPS. One crew keeps pointing at the MOB to provide visual reference for helm. Throw the danbuoy and horseshoe lifebelt as soon as possible.

2 Heave to' by coming up to the wind and tacking, leaving the headsail backed and hauling the mainsheet in as close as possible.

3 Sail on beam reach, and if sufficient wind to maintain way under mainsail alone, drop the headsails. Allow yourself sea room to manoeuvre and tack, but don't let the MOB go out of sight.

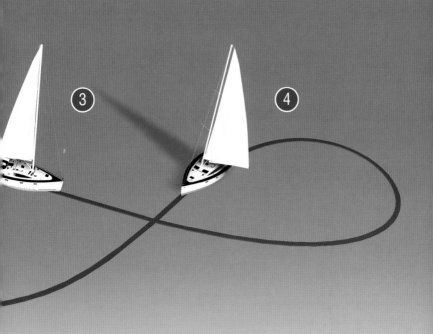

4. Sail far enough downwind to be able to approach the MOB on a fine reach. This allows you to maintain control and stop easily by de-powering the mainsail. Sail towards the MOB. De-power the mainsail by releasing the kicking strap and letting the sheet out until the sail flaps. The rescuing party must be forward of the shrouds so as not to be injured by the boom.

5. If you are sailing in at too tight an angle, duck sharply downwind for 3 boat lengths and point up again at the MOB once the mainsail can be de-powered.

6. Approach the MOB on a fine reach, easing the sheet in the final stages. Leeway will increase as you slow down. Recover the MOB on leeward side of the yacht.

First Aid

Seasickness

This is the most common form on illness onboard and there are some people who should simply never go afloat. They have the misfortune to suffer motion sickness sitting in the back seat of a car just as much as on a boat. They know who they are and shouldn't be encouraged to do something they know they will regret. Others find they become affected only for a short time. Many succumb only when it is rough. The lucky few remain immune whatever the weather or sickening antics of those around them.

The are all manner of remedies from Scopolamine patches stuck behind the ear and pressure padded wrist straps to anti-sickness pills such as Cinnarlilzine and Prochlorherazine. Non-alcohlic ginger wine, fizzy water and dry crackers also help settle the tummy and will keep you from dehydrating. If you are a sufferer, try them all to find which works best.

A selection of remedies to ward off seasickness. Try them all to find which works best for you.

Here are a few tips that may help

- Start medication 12 hours before you sail

- Avoid alcohol and strong tastes the night before

- Get plenty of rest

- Keep warm

- Stay on deck

- Keep an eye on the horizon. This can help your brain recalibrate your equilibrium

- Steering, keeping active on deck or lying down below (with a bucket near to hand) all help to hold back seasickness

- Avoid:
  - Cooking
  - Eating
  - Diesel fumes
  - Working on the engine in a confined space
  - Writing

First Aid kit

The longer you are at sea, the better stocked the first aid kit needs to be. If you are limited to cruising inshore, then a small domestic first-aid kit will suffice. This should be stored in a waterproof case.

If you are planning a weekend or week-long voyage then more comprehensive medical supplies are required.

TIME AT SEA		MEDICATIONS	USE FOR
2 DAYS	3-7 DAYS		
Antibiotics for infections			
✓	✓	Erythyrmycin	Skin infections
✓	✓	Ciprofloxacin	Various infections
Analgesics for pain			
✓	✓	Aspirin/Paracetamol	For mild pain, fever and sunburn
✓	✓	Ibuprofen	For moderate pain
✓	✓	Ibuprofen gel	To rub on sprains and strains
Acute anxiety/fits/sleeplessness			
	✓	Diazepam	Anxiety and fits
Ears			
✓	✓	Otomixe (ear spray)	Infections, ear canal
Eyes			
✓	✓	Chloramaphenicol	Conjunctivitis
✓	✓	Hydrocortisone	Allergic red eye
Mouth and throat			
	✓	Bonjela	Mouth ulcers
✓	✓	Throat lozenges	Sore throats

TIME AT SEA		MEDICATIONS	USE FOR
2 DAYS	3-7 DAYS		
	✓	Prednisolone	Anaphylactic shock and asthma
✓	✓	Chlorpheniramine	Watery eyes, runny nose caused by allergies, hay fever, and the common cold
	✓	Salbutamol	Allergies above and asthma
Stomach and gut			
✓	✓	Gaviscon	Indigestion
	✓	Omeprazole	Severe peptic ulcer pain
✓	✓	Cinnarizine/Scopolamine (patches)	Seasickness
✓	✓	Loperamide	Diarrhoea
	✓	Bisacodyl	Constipation
	✓	Anusol	Piles
✓	✓	Dioralyte	Salt and fluid replacement
Skin preparations			
✓	✓	E45	Dry skin
✓	✓	Hydrocortisone	Rashes
✓	✓	Zinc	Salt water sores
	✓	Miconazole	Foot and crotch rot
	✓	Flamazine	Burns
✓	✓	Acicelovir	Cold sores
	✓	Sterzac	To dry wet rashes
✓	✓	Vaseline	General skin protection
✓	✓	Calamine	Sunburn
✓	✓	Chlorehxidine	Skin disinfectant

TIME AT SEA		MEDICATIONS	USE FOR
2 DAYS	3-7 DAYS		
Anesthetic agents			
✓	✓	Lignocaine (injection)	Before suturing/ stapling
Cardiac agents			
✓	✓	Glycerol trinitrate spray	To increase heart circulation
General supplies			
✓	✓	Head torch	
✓	✓	Strong scissors	
✓	✓	Pocket resuscitation mask	
✓	✓	Flexible probe, digital thermometer	
	✓	Naso-pharyngeal airways	
✓	✓	Sam splint	
	✓	Fracture straps (Velco)	
	✓	Adjustable cervical collar	
✓	✓	Thermal protection aids	
	✓	Skin stapler and remover	
✓	✓	Skin closure strips	
	✓	Dermabond skin glue	
✓	✓	Eye irrigation bottle	
	✓	Dental kit	
✓	✓	Safety pins	

TIME AT SEA		MEDICATIONS	USE FOR
2 DAYS	3-7 DAYS		
✓	✓	Magnifying glass	
✓	✓	Scalpel and blades	
✓	✓	Tongue depressors	
✓	✓	Eye pads and patches	
✓	✓	Slings (triangular bandages)	
✓	✓	Sterile gauze	
✓	✓	Field dressings	
✓	✓	Tubi grip and applicator	
✓	✓	Elastoplasts	
✓	✓	Cling film	
✓	✓	Gaffa tape	
	✓	Burns kit	
✓	✓	Crepe bandages	
	✓	Cling and conforming gauze bandages	
✓	✓	Melanin wound dressings	
✓	✓	Microspore tape bandages	
✓	✓	Cotton wool	
✓	✓	Cotton buds	
	✓	Ribbon gauze	
	✓	Instant ice pack	

Useful addresses

Admiralty Easytide predictions: easytide.ukho.gov.uk

Association of Marine Electronic and Radio Colleges (AMERC)
www.amerc.ac.uk
National helpline: +44 (0) 1539 440218

DWD Marine forecast: weather.mailasail.com

European Health Insurance Card (EHIC): www.ehic.uk.com
National helpline: +44 (0) 845 606 2030
E-mail: info@ehic.uk.com

HM Revenue and Customs: customs.hmrc.gov.uk
National helpline: +44 (0) 845 010 9000
National yachtline: +44 (0) 845 723 1110

Maritime and Coastguard Agency: www.mcga.gov.uk
Emergency tel: 999

Met Office: www.metoffice.gov.uk
National helpline: +44 (0) 870 900 0100
From overseas:+44 1392 885680

Ofcom Radio Licensing Centre: www.ofcom.org.uk/licensing
National helpline: +44 (0) 20 7981 3131
E-mail: licensingcentre@ofcom.org.uk

Pet Travel Scheme: www.defra.gov.uk
National helpline: +44 (0) 870 241 1710
E-mail: quarantine@animalhealth.gsi.gov.uk

Register of British Ships: www.mcga.gov.uk
National helpline: +44 (0) 29 2044 8813

Royal Yachting Association (RYA): www.rya.org.uk
National helpline:+44 (0) 845 345 0400

UK Border Agency: www.bia.homeoffice.gov.uk
National helpline: +44 (0) 845 010 5200
E-mail: ukbanationalityenquiries@ukba.gsi.gov.uk

UK Hydrographic Office: www.ukho.gov.uk
National helpline: +44 (0) 1823 284077
Notices to mariners: noticestomariners@ukho.gov.uk

Sailing Directions: +44 (0) 1823 337900 ext 3382
E-mail: sailingdirections@ukho.gov.uk

Tides helpline: +44 (0) 1823 337900 ext 3533/3530
E-mail: tides@ukho.gov.uk

HM Coastguard Maritime Rescue Co-ordination Centres

Aberdeen – *Cape Wrath to Doonies Point*
4th Floor, Marine House, Blaikies Quay, Aberdeen, AB11 5PB
Tel: +44 (0) 1224 592334

Belfast – *Northern Ireland/Irish Republic border, Lough*
Bregenz House, Quay Street, Bangor, Co Down, BT20 5ED
Tel: +44 (0) 2891 463933

Brixham – *Topsham to Dodman Point*
Kings Quay, Brixham, Devon, TQ5 9TW
Tel: +44 (0) 1803 882704

Clyde – *Mull of Galloway to Ardmurchan Point including the Islands of Jura, Gigha, Islay, Arran, Colonsay, Coll, Tiree, Mull, Bute, and Cumbrae*
Navy Buildings, Eldon Street, Greenock, Inverclyde, PA16 7QY
Tel: +44 (0) 1475 729988

Dover – *Reculver Towers to Beachy Head*
Langdon Battery, Swingate, Dover, Kent, CT15 5NA
Tel: +44 (0) 1304 210008

Falmouth – *Marsland Mouth – Devon border to Dodman Point*
Pendennis Point, Castle Drive, Falmouth, TR11 4WZ
Tel: +44 (0) 1326 317575

Forth – *Doonies Point to Berwick on Tweed*
Fifeness, Crail, Fife, KY10 3XN
Tel: +44 (0) 1333 450666

Holyhead – *Froig to Queensferry*
Prince of Wales Road, Holyhead, Anglesey, North Wales, LL26 1ET
Tel: +44 (0) 1407 762051/763911

Humber – *Scottish border to Haile Sand Fort*
Limekiln Lane, Bridlington, East Yorkshire, YO15 2LX
Tel: 01262 672317

Liverpool – *Queensferry to the Mull of Galloway, Scotland, plus the English Lake District*
Hall Road West, Crosby, Liverpool, L23 8SY
Tel: +44 (0) 1519 313341

London – *River Thames from Shell Haven Point to Teddington*
Thames Barrier Navigation Centre, 34 Bowater Road, Woolwich, SE18 5TF
Tel: +44 (0) 2083 127380

Milford Haven – *Camarthen to Froig*
Gorsewood Drive, Hakin, Milford Haven, Pemrokeshire, SA73 3HB
Tel: +44 (0) 1646 690909

Portland – *Dorset/Hampshire border to Topsham*
Custom House Quay, Weymouth, Dorset, DT4 8BE
Tel: +44 (0) 1305 760439

Shetland – *Shetland Islands Fair Isle and the Orkney Islands*
The Knab, Knab Road, Lerwick, Shetland, ZE1 0AX
Tel: +44 (0) 1595 692976

Solent – *Dorset/Hampshire border to Beachy Head including the Isle of Wight*
44A Marine Parade West, Lee On Solent, Hampshire, PO13 9NR
Tel: +44 (0) 2392 552100

Stornoway – *Ardnamurchan Point to Cape Wrath, Mainland – Barra Head to Butt of Lewis and St Kilda*
Clan Macquarrie House, Battery Point, Stornoway, Isle of Lewis, Western Isles, HS1 2RT
Tel: +44 (0) 1851 702013/4

Swansea – *Marsland Mouth, North Devon to River Towy, Camarthen*
Tutt Head, Mumbles, Swansea, SA3 4EX
Tel: +44 (0) 1792 366534

Thames – *Southwold to Herne Bay*
East Terrace, Walton on Naze, Essex, CO14 8PY
Tel: +44 (0) 1255 675518

Yarmouth – *Haile Sand Fort to Southwold*
Havenbridge House, North Quay, Great Yarmouth, Norfolk, NR30 1HZ
Tel: +44 (0) 1493 851338

International Code of Signals and morse code symbols

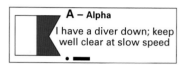

A – Alpha
I have a diver down; keep well clear at slow speed
• ▬

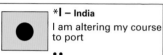

*I – India
I am altering my course to port
• •

*B – Bravo
I am taking in, or discharging, or carrying dangerous goods
▬ • • •

J – Juliett
I am on fire and have dangerous cargo; keep well clear of me
• ▬ ▬ ▬

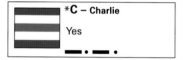

*C – Charlie
Yes
▬ • ▬ •

K – Kilo
I wish to communicate with you
▬ • ▬

*D – Delta
Keep clear of me; I am manoeuvring with difficulty
▬ • •

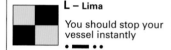

L – Lima
You should stop your vessel instantly
• ▬ • •

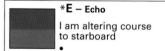

*E – Echo
I am altering course to starboard
•

*M – Mike
My vessel is stopped and making no way through the water
▬ ▬

F – Foxtrot
I am disabled; communicate with me
• • ▬ •

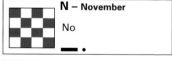

N – November
No
▬ •

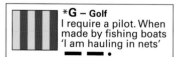

*G – Golf
I require a pilot. When made by fishing boats 'I am hauling in nets'
▬ ▬ •

O – Oscar
Man overboard

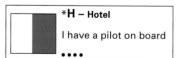

*H – Hotel
I have a pilot on board
• • • •

P – Papa
Vessel about to put to sea. By fishing vessels 'My nets are caught fast'
• ▬ ▬ •

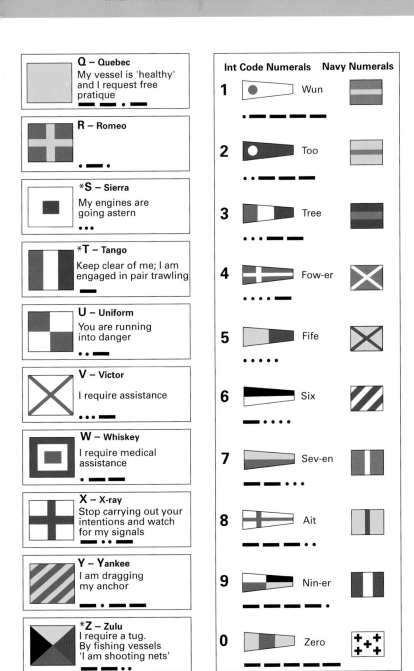

Q – Quebec
My vessel is 'healthy' and I request free pratique

R – Romeo

*S – Sierra
My engines are going astern

*T – Tango
Keep clear of me; I am engaged in pair trawling

U – Uniform
You are running into danger

V – Victor
I require assistance

W – Whiskey
I require medical assistance

X – X-ray
Stop carrying out your intentions and watch for my signals

Y – Yankee
I am dragging my anchor

*Z – Zulu
I require a tug.
By fishing vessels 'I am shooting nets'

Int Code Numerals   **Navy Numerals**

1   Wun

2   Too

3   Tree

4   Fow-er

5   Fife

6   Six

7   Sev-en

8   Ait

9   Nin-er

0   Zero

Useful publications

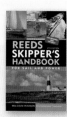

Reeds Skipper's Handbook (6th edition)
by Malcolm Pearson
ISBN 978 1 4081 2477 2 · £7.99

In handy pocket size, an aide-memoire of everything a boater needs to know at sea. Packed with useful information in concise form, it is frequently recommended by Yachtmaster Instructors as a quick reference guide and as a revision aid for anyone taking their Day Skipper and Yachtmaster certificates.

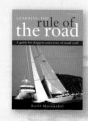

Learning the Rule of the Road (4th edition)
A Guide for the Skippers and
Crew of Small Craft
by Basil Mosenthal
ISBN 978 1 4081 0633 4 · £10.99

This guide clearly and simply explains the International Regulations for Preventing Collisions at Sea, looking particularly at those sections affecting small craft. Ideal for beginners or as an aide-memoire for those with more experience.

Skipper's Cockpit Guide (2nd edition)
Instant Facts and Practical Hints for Boaters
by Bo Streiffert
ISBN 978 0 7136 8753 8 · £9.99

This quick reference guide contains all the navigational information and practical seamanship needed by skippers or crew. The accessible and concise presentation makes it ideal for instant reference at sea, and its splash-proof pages and spiral binding enable it to stand up to the demanding marine environment.

Yachtsman's Ten Language Dictionary
(3rd edition)
English, French, German, Dutch, Danish,
Spanish, Italian, Portuguese, Turkish, Greek
by Barbara Webb and Cruising Association
ISBN 978 0 7136 8440 7 · £17.99

The third edition of this multilingual dictionary has been revised and updated to take into account the developments in electrical and mechanical equipment, GRP boat construction and the cruising patterns of charter, flotilla and cruising skippers. Ideal for all your boating terms.

Yachtsman's Tidal Atlas
Channel Ports and Approaches
by Michael Reeve-Fowkes
ISBN 978 0 7136 6729 5 · £9.99

This easy-to-read tidal atlas includes comprehensive and detailed tidal streams and tidal heights and an annual Cherbourg tide table. It covers The Solent and Approaches, Portland Bill, Alderney and Cherbourg, Poole, Russell Channels, St Helier Approaches, St Malo Approaches, Ile de Brehat, Le Havre, The Scilly Isles, Ile d'Ouessant and Chenal du Four.

Yachtsman's Tidal Atlas
Southern North Sea & Eastern Channel
by Michael Reeve-Fowkes
ISBN 978 0 9487 8837 6 · £9.99

This comprehensive tidal atlas includes detailed tidal streams and tidal heights in an accessible format with clear data. It includes an annual Cherbourg tide table and covers the Solent to the Wash and Cherbourg to Den Helder.

Index

Magical moments during a cross-Channel cruise – dolphins playing in the bow wave.